ICE HOCKEY

AND ICE POLO

GUIDE

CONTAINING A COMPLETE RECORD OF THE SEASON OF
1896-97, WITH AMENDED PLAYING RULES OF

THE AMATEUR HOCKEY LEAGUE of NEW YORK,
THE AMATEUR HOCKEY ASSOCIATION of
CANADA, THE ONTARIO HOCKEY AS-
SOCIATION and NEW ENGLAND
SKATING ASSOCIATION -
ICE POLO LEAGUE

EDITED AND COMPILED BY J. A. TUTHILL
MONTCLAIR ATHLETIC CLUB

W. P. Grant.   MacDougal.   W. Jack (Hon. Vice-Pres.)
Gillelan.   de Sterneck.   Grant (Capt.) Henderson. Wilson (Pres.)   McLea.
Drinkwater.   Davidson.   Meredith (Hon. Pres.) R. E. MacDougal.

VICTORIA HOCKEY CLUB, OF MONTREAL.

Champions of the World, 1897.   Senior Champions of Amateur Hockey League of Canada, Season of 1897.

ICE HOCKEY.

*

HISTORICAL AND DESCRIPTIVE.

Ice hockey is fast becoming a regulation American sport.
Like many others it is an imported pastime and has found
almost as much favor during the past winter as did golf after
the first year of its introduction. Along with the revival of
indoor athletics has come an increased interest in ice hockey,
which, dating back but a couple of years, last winter amounted
to that purely American outburst of effort known as a "boom."
Three winters ago Chicago, Minneapolis and Detroit were
about the only scenes of the game's activity, but last winter
wherever ice could be found, out of doors or inside, East and
West, ice hockey was being played.

The game should not be confused with hockey nor ice polo.
The former (from which ice hockey and ice polo have grown)
is a very ancient field pastime, sometimes known as bandy,
shinney or shintey.   Originally, Romans played the game with
a leather ball stuffed with feathers and a crooked club or bat
called a bandy, because of being bent.   A fourteenth century
manuscript contains a drawing of two bandy players facing
each other at a short distance and armed with bandy sticks,
very similar to the hockey sticks of the present day used in the
United Kingdom.   The object was to strike the ball past each
other, and if one failed to stop it, whatever ground was covered
by the ball was claimed by the opponent, and so on with varying success until either boundary was reached, the latter being
the goal.

Logan (Sec.)   Howe.   Bruce.   MacDonald.
        White.   Strong.   Nixon (Pres.)   Robinson.   Boswell.   Code (V.-Pres.)
    Johnston.   Campbell.   Armytage (Capt.)   Howard.   Benson.
                        Merritt.   Bain.

VICTORIA HOCKEY CLUB, WINNIPEG.

Senior and Intermediate Champions, Manitoba and Northwest Amateur Hockey Association, Season
1896-97.   Seniors—Buffalo Emblem; Intermediates—V Emblem.

The game (hockey) which is now very popular in Great Britain is played on a rectangular field of turf, 125 yards long by 54 yards wide, with goal posts quite similar to those we use for foot ball. Fifteen players constitute a team, which consists of a goal-keeper, two backs, three half-backs, seven forwards and two advance-forwards. They carry ash sticks 34 inches or less in length, with a crook at the lower end not more than four inches long, and endeavor to strike a self-inflating one-ounce india rubber ball (which is 1¾ inches in diameter) with the stick, so as to make it pass between the goal posts and under the cross bar. As may be imagined, the game is exceedingly rough, probably because so many men are bunched at times. From this British game Canadians extracted ice hockey and have played the game so long in their climate, where natural ice skating is indulged in steadily from Dec. 1st until late in each spring, that they have well nigh reached perfection.

Only in the most northerly part of the United States are the winters severe enough to make ice hockey very practicable out of doors. (Every Canadian town of ordinary size has its covered, natural-ice rink.) In other parts of our country the lakes and rivers are seldom frozen hard enough for skating or ice sports for any length of time, and this has caused a number of artificial-ice rinks to be constructed in our big cities, where most of the ice hockey matches are played.

The sport has flourished with both the player and spectator and will be found interesting to the most exacting critic, his attention being fully occupied through every moment of play. It has all the rapidity and great variety of action to be seen in lacrosse and polo (on horseback) without the roughness of the former or danger of the latter, and the same opportunity is offered for individual, brilliant play and perfect team-work (the secret of an ice hockey team's success). From the moment the referee signifies the start, the spectators' nerves are kept at a tension which is not relaxed until the final call of time, there being very little or nothing of the element of "time calls," which have proved such a fruitful cause for criticism in foot ball. Occasionally a skate may be broken, necessitating a

Cotton.   Baker.   Hicks.   Deal.
Weller.   Kennard.   H. Whitehurst. M. Whitehurst. Charbonnel
Pond. (Capt. & Mgr.)

UNIVERSITY OF MARYLAND ICE HOCKEY TEAM.

Champions of Baltimore Hockey League, 1896-97.

delay of five minutes, but this occurs rarely; or a player insisting on continued off-side play or being sent from the ice for infringement of any rule, causing a momentary stoppage. Otherwise the time is employed in brilliant rushes, quick checking and clever passes.

The requisites are few—a clear sheet of hard ice, invigorating atmosphere and a number of quick, sure skaters, who, when aided and abetted by an enthusiastic company of supporters, will furnish as interesting an evening's entertainment as any sport lover could desire. The principles of the game are so simple as to be readily understood by even the most disinterested. An ice hockey team is composed of seven men, four of whom are called forwards or rushers and form the attack, while the other three, cover-point, point and goal-keeper, have only defensive work, though at intervals the cover-point is called upon to back up or feed the forwards. Goal posts are erected at either end of a rink, shaped like a foot ball or lacrosse field, which is bounded by upright planking, touching and extending two or more feet in height from the ice surface. Each player is equipped with a "stick," made preferably of second-growth ash, length to suit holder, resembling in form somewhat an ice polo stick, except it is not so curved on the end, which is formed into a blade less than thirteen inches in length and three in width, and bent so as to rest and allow about a foot of play along the ice. The object is to drive the "puck" between and through the opponents' goal posts. The puck is a disk of solid vulcanized rubber three inches in diameter and one inch thick. It slides along the ice with great ease and rapidity, being usually dribbled, and as it passes from player to player it is shoved or scooped rather than struck at.

A successful ice hockey player must be very active on his feet, quick with his hand, keen of eye and have all his faculties alert. He must be an expert on skates, as almost every known skill on ice is needed in the game, and he should be mounted on regulation ice hockey skates, the blades of which are almost straight on the bottom and thus better adapted for the light-

D. Bain.   R. Benson.   R. M. Flett.
C. J. Campbell. J. C. G. Armytage G. H. Merritt.
F. Higginbotham.   (Capt.).   T. A. Howard.
A. Code, Vice-Pres.   J. Carter (Mascot).   E. B. Nixon, Pres.

VICTORIA ICE HOCKEY TEAM OF WINNIPEG.

ning turns and sudden stops necessary in the play. He must be able to start quickly and to skate fast and low—as a back must run "hard and low" in foot ball—thus preventing being easily thrown off his feet by the body-checking, blocking or interference (all of which is allowed) of an opponent. He must be able to twist and dodge quickly, as it is often useful in outwitting an opponent who blocks the path toward the goal. An accomplishment much practiced in Canada, and a very useful one, too, is jumping over the stick of an opponent while under full headway, and thus avoiding many a fall or, trip, intentional or otherwise. As ice hockey is a very severe game and one that calls for constant exertion, on the part of the forwards in particular, players must be athletes of exceptional endurance and have any amount of grit and "sand."

Two halves of thirty (sometimes twenty) minutes each constitute time of play, and the game is in charge of a referee, two goal umpires and one or two timekeepers.

The play is started by "facing" the puck at the centre of the field between the sticks of two opposing centre forwards. When the referee calls "play" these men strive to gain possession of the puck and pass it to other players of their own team and an exciting attack and defense of goals follows. Of the four forwards the two best goal-drivers should hold centre positions and the fastest forwards be placed in the wings or on the ends. As soon as one of the four gains possession of the puck he rushes for the goal his team is attacking, the remaining three following close behind or abreast of him, but spread out *across* the rink in an irregular line. Where good form is shown, one forward rarely carries the puck longer than a few seconds, it being kept on the pass from one to the other with great speed and accuracy, thus lessening the opportunity for an opponent to gain its possession. On their way toward the goal—granted that the opposing forwards have been passed— the opposing cover-point is the first man encountered and he, of course, confronts the player with the puck. The latter passes it across to one of his partners and thus they advance until the point is reached, where perhaps another pass is neces-

Sutton. Ryder. Hall. Sheldon. Barnes. Barnett. Walworth. Stoddard. Smith.
(Capt.)

YALE UNIVERSITY ICE HOCKEY TEAM, 1896-97.

sary and, if successful, the goal is attacked. A number of quick shots and stops follow until a goal is either scored, or an opponent "lifts" the puck down the rink and out of harm's way, or possibly dribbles it down, followed by his own forwards and thus forms the attacking party on the other goal.

The sides of the rink are used somewhat like billiard cushions, and in making a run, a player will, after having used his ability in dodging his opponents, carrom the puck past an opponent, or to another of his own side who has signaled and is ready to receive it. While running with the puck it should be dribbled just ahead of the player; that is, advanced by a rapid succession of short, alternate right and left strokes, thus baffling an attacking opponent.

The main object of an expert player, and very difficult of accomplishment, is to "lift" the puck, making it travel over the heads of his opponents a distance of twenty or thirty yards perhaps when necessary before striking the ice. It is the duty of the point and cover-point to "lift" whenever necessary to keep the puck in the vicinity of the opposition goal. These two players are "feeders" for their forwards, and they should "run" down *with* the puck when they have fairly clear ice, rather than losing possession of it by lifting. This stroke is also invaluable to a player when shooting for goal, as a goal keeper can almost always stop the puck when shot from any distance if it slides along the ice with his skates or stick, but they are of little use in preventing a sizzling, "lifted" shot from scoring which comes at the goal about two feet from the ice. To "lift" a puck, an indescribable wrist motion or twist is imparted to the stroke, which employs a full arm and body motion to give it force, and it can only be gained by long practice. An expert can "lift" a puck through the air with the greatest accuracy and terrific speed. Of course, both hands are used to handle the stick—this being an unwritten law of ice hockey—and a player need never expect to do *any* effective work without both hands on his stick at *any* stage of the play. A player who attempts to advance or even control a puck with but one hand on his stick, and the latter probably at arm's

G. Curtis.

R. Hiscock. J. Harty (Capt.) G. Dalton.
W. Merrill. F. Weatherhead. R. Brock.

QUEENS UNIVERSITY HOCKEY TEAM.

length, is easily disposed of by an adversary, who can readily
push the one-hander's stick away by the slightest blow, whereas,
if properly held, a much greater degree of force can be with-
stood, and the control is strengthened beyond measure.

The "off-side" rule in ice hockey is the controlling feature
of the game, adding to the play great interest and complete
government of attacking methods. The rule provides that a
player shall always be on his own side of the puck or simply
speaking, its object is to prevent a player passing the puck
forward to *another member of his own team*, but admits of his
passing it across the rink at right angles to the side lines, or
back toward his own goal. A player is "off-side" if he is
nearer the opponent's goal line than the player of his own team
who last hit the puck, and he is not allowed to touch it, or
interfere or obstruct an opponent until again "on-side." He
may be put "on-side" when the puck has been touched by an
opponent, or when he has skated back of one of his own side
who either has possession of the puck or played it last when
behind the offender. A match is stopped if a man, when off-
side, plays the puck or obstructs an opponent, and as a penalty
the puck is faced where it was last played from before the infringement occurred.*

This rule tends to make the player in possession of the puck
keep even with or a trifle ahead of his other forwards at all
times, thus allowing him to pass it to any of them whenever
his progress may be threatened or obstructed; were they ahead
of him he would be without allies.

The puck may only be advanced by the use of the stick, but
it may be stopped by the skate or any part of the body (the
Ontario Hockey Association rules prevent stopping the puck
with the hand except by the goal-tend). Thus a clever goal-
tend intercepts many a try-for-goal, though at the cost of as
many bruises where his body has met the flying puck. He

* The rules of the Amateur Hockey League of New York, enforced last
winter, provided for the surrender of the puck to the opposing side in the
event of an off-side play, the offending team not being allowed to approach
nearer than five yards while the puck was being put in play again without
interference. This rule has now been made void.

Stackhouse. Agnew. Orton. Decker.
Phymester. H. Gibbons M. Gibbons Chattin. Stanley.
(Capt.) (Mgr.)
Gosman. Moore.

UNIVERSITY OF PENNSYLVANIA HOCKEY TEAM.

very rarely leaves his station between the goal-posts, and then only after signaling the point to fall back into his position, the goal-tend having left same in order to return a long "lift" which has dropped back of and near the posts, the opposing forwards, of course, being at some distance down the rink.

Through the agility of a clever goal-tend the score of a match is often kept down to a small number of goals, as he kills many tries which would score but for his good work. The rules forbid him to lie, sit or kneel upon the ice, and compel him to maintain a standing position. When a scrimmage occurs near his goal, his is the most difficult, and usually the most thankless, work of any man on the team. Though he may frequently gain a momentary possession of the puck, he seldom has room or time to pass it far down the rink or even directly to one of his own side. His play then is to shoot it off to one side of the rink, either to the right or left of the goal, thus preventing another try-for-goal until the puck is worked back again into a favorable position.

The thorough or loose work of a referee regulates the amount of foul play in ice hockey, and unless he be firm and strict, for players so inclined, there are many opportunities to trip, collar, kick, push, cross-check, charge from behind, etc., all of which are forbidden by the rules. For infringements of this character, as well as for raising a stick above the shoulder, the penalty is disqualification, the referee ruling the offending player off the ice, for any portion of actual playing time as he may deem fit.

Goal umpiring is by no means the least important part of an ice hockey match, though the manner in which this office was filled at many league contests in New York City last winter would lead one so to believe. As a decision made by a goal umpire is final, he should be most painstaking and always on the alert. His work can only be performed properly when stationed in a cleared space reserved solely for his use. This space should be just back of the rink boundary and somewhat longer than the goal is wide, as he must be able to move instantly in order to get a true line on shots for goal made at

B. Bogert. Bartow S. Weeks, D. M. Spaulding. E. J. Giannini, A. G. Fry. F. S. Wonham.
Captain.   Ath. Director.
I. A. Lynch.   J. A. Fenwick,   G. B. Macrae.
Team Captain.

NEW YORK ATHLETIC CLUB HOCKEY TEAM.

Champions of Amateur Hockey League of New York, 1896–'97.

many different angles. Many a match has been won for a team by the tricky work of their goal tend, who by a quick stroke has put the puck in play again after having stopped it several inches in goal, this being done of course when a "slow" umpire was "taking things easy" in a chair directly behind the goal-tend's back, or caught standing in a similar position.

Wood.   Ellison.   Banning.   Gottlieb (Mgr.)   Kelly.   Cornell.   Kahn.
            Longfield.   Canoll   Tower (Capt.)   Wood.
                    ICE PALACE ICE POLO CLUB, 1895-95.

A REVIEW OF ICE HOCKEY DURING THE WINTER OF 1896-97

❧

GREATER NEW YORK.

In New York City ice hockey made its greatest strides during the past winter, and met with much favor from the public. The progress of the game was mainly due to the fact that three artificial-ice rinks were maintained in and about the city, a privilege which many localities have not enjoyed. The New York Hockey Club, now known as the Hockey Club of New York, which is composed entirely of Canadian residents of the metropolis, who learned the game on the other side of the St. Lawrence River, was the first to introduce ice hockey in New York. During the winter of '95-'96 they practiced regularly at the "Ice Palace" Rink, where they made their headquarters, and played several matches with the Montclair Athletic Club team and two visiting teams from Montreal, and also the Baltimore Athletic Club team. During the close of the season (in the latter part of March, '96) the St. Nicholas Rink was opened, and with it came the organization of the St. Nicholas Skating Club and its hockey team. The latter club met and defeated representative teams from Cornell and Yale Universities, but lost to the New York Hockey Club, who were without doubt entitled to the championship honor of the season.

This crack team of New York Hockey Club experts, some of whom were previously members of the New York Athletic Club, all became identified with the latter club early last winter, and as representatives of this powerful athletic organization again won the undisputed title of champions ; this time, however, of the Amateur Hockey League as well.

A. S. Williams.   A. Kennaday.   H. J. Koehler (Capt.)   E. J. Emerson.
H. Hornfeck.   J. A. Tuthill (Mgr.)   G. Hornfeck.   M. Hornfeck.

MONTCLAIR ATHLETIC CLUB HOCKEY TEAM, 1896–97.

This league was formed in November, '96, and included the New York Athletic Club, St. Nicholas Skating Club, Crescent Athletic Club, and Skating Club of Brooklyn. The two latter clubs represented the Clermont Avenue Rink in Brooklyn, the St. Nicholas Rink being the home ice of the remaining two. A series of matches was inaugurated, and play continued throughout the winter for a championship trophy. The matches resulted as follows :

AMATEUR HOCKEY LEAGUE OF NEW YORK—RECORD OF MATCHES—SEASON OF 1896-97.

Date		Goals		Goals
Dec. 16	St. Nicholas S. C.	16	S. C. of Brooklyn	0
Dec. 22	New York A. C.	22	Crescent A. C.	0
Jan. 5	New York A. C.	14	S. C. of Brooklyn	0
Jan. 14	St. Nicholas S. C.	7	Crescent A. C.	0
Jan. 26	S. C. of Brooklyn	2	Crescent A. C.	2
Jan. 30	New York A. C.	3	St. Nicholas S. C.	2
Feb. 16	New York A. C.	11	Crescent A. C.	0
Feb. 23	St. Nicholas S. C.	8	S. C. of Brooklyn	0
*Feb. 26	S. C. of Brooklyn	7	Crescent A. C.	0
March 2	New York A. C.	7	S. C. of Brooklyn	1
March 4	St. Nicholas S. C.	10	Crescent A. C.	1
March 9	S. C. of Brooklyn	3	Crescent A. C.	0
March 23	New York A. C.	3	St. Nicholas S. C.	1

*Play off of tie match of Jan. 26th.

SUMMARY BY MATCHES.

	Won	Lost	Tied
New York Athletic Club	6	0	0
St. Nicholas Skating Club	4	2	0
Skating Club of Brooklyn	2	4	1
Crescent Athletic Club	0	6	1

SUMMARY BY GOALS.

	Scored	Opponents Scored
New York Athletic Club	60	4
St. Nicholas Skating Club	44	7
Skating Club of Brooklyn	13	47
Crescent Athletic Club	3	62

NOTE.—On April 2d an exhibition game was played at the St. Nicholas Rink between the St. Nicholas and New York A. C. teams. The latter played several substitutes and lost by a score of one goal to none.

As the summary shows, the New York A. C. team won quite easily, the only competitors who forced them in the least being the St. Nicholas team. The two clubs from Brooklyn were never in the hunt at any stage of the game, the form they exhibited being far out-pointed by many minor teams whom they met in exhibition matches throughout the winter.

A. Griffen.   C. Phillips.   W. McBurney.   C. Anderson.   R. Trautschold.
A. Lindley.   G. Hornfeck.   E. Cary.

MONTCLAIR HIGH SCHOOL HOCKEY TEAM, 1897.

SOME PROMINENT EXHIBITION MATCHES PLAYED BY THE TEAMS OF THE AMATEUR HOCKEY LEAGUE DURING THE SEASON OF 1896-97.

Date	Where Played		Goals		Goals
Dec. 12	St. Nicholas Rink	New York A. C.	4	New York Hockey Club	1
Dec. 18	Ice Palace Rink	New York A. C.	1	New York Hockey Club	1
Dec. 24	St. Nicholas Rink	St. Nicholas S. C.	3	Yale University	2
Dec. 29	Clermont Rink	Crescent A. C.	5	Montclair A. C.	5
Jan. 2	St. Nicholas Rink	St. Nicholas S. C.	1	New York Hockey Club	1
Jan. 8	Ice Palace Rink	Crescent A. C.	1	New York Hockey Club	1
Jan. 8	Clermont Rink	Skating Club of Brooklyn	0	Columbia University	10
Jan. 13*	St. Nicholas Rink	New York A. C.	1	Yale University	0
Jan. 8	St. Nicholas Rink	New York A. C.	7	Princeton University	1
Jan. 15	Clermont Rink	Skating Club of Brooklyn	3	Montclair A. C.	0
Jan. 21	St. Nicholas Rink	Skating Club of Brooklyn	3	New York Hockey Club	2
Jan. 22	St. Nicholas Rink	New York A. C.	2	Orange Lake Ice Yacht Club	0
Jan. 23	Clermont Rink	Skating Club of Brooklyn	7	Queens University, Canada	1
Jan. 25	St. Nicholas Rink	St. Nicholas S. C.	1	South Orange Field Club	2
Jan. 29	Clermont Rink	Skating Club of Brooklyn	1	South Orange Field Club	1
Feb. 3	St. Nicholas Rink	New York A. C.	8	New York Hockey Club	1
Feb. 5	Ice Palace Rink	Skating Club of Brooklyn	0	Cambridge (Mass.) Hockey Team	1
Feb. 9	St. Nicholas Rink	St. Nicholas S. C.	2	Cambridge (Mass.) Hockey Team	1
Feb. 11	St. Nicholas Rink	New York A. C.	1	Princeton University	2
Feb. 11	Clermont Rink	Skating Club of Brooklyn	0	Yale University	0
Feb. 13	St. Nicholas Rink	New York A. C.	5	Yale University	0
Feb. 20	St. Nicholas Rink	New York A. C.	5	Yale University (Class of '97)	0
Feb. 27	Crescent A. C.	Crescent A. C.	2	Maryland A. C.	0
March 3	Baltimore (Md.) Rink	St. Nicholas S. C.	8	Mountain Toboggan Club of Orange, N. J.	3
March 5	Clermont Rink	Crescent A. C.	3	Montclair A. C.	3
March 6	Clermont Rink	Skating Club of Brooklyn	11	Second Division, First Naval Battalion, S N. Y.	0
March 6	St. Nicholas Rink	St. Nicholas S. C.	5	University of Maryland	1
March 9	Baltimore (Md.) Rink	New York A. C.	1	Montclair A. C.	0
March 18	St. Nicholas Rink	St. Nicholas S. C.	3	Yale University	0
April 1	St. Nicholas Rink	St. Nicholas S. C.	8	Second Division, First Naval Battalion, S.N.Y.	1
*April 2	St. Nicholas Rink	St. Nicholas S. C.	1	New York A. C.	0

* Not a league match. See note, page 28.

Mackey.   Genert.   Gordon.   *
   Walton.   Cooper.   S. Brown.
   Banister.   Borland.   N. Day.

NEW JERSEY A. C. ICE HOCKEY TEAM.

The personnel of the four teams of the Amateur Hockey League was as follows:

NEW YORK ATHLETIC CLUB.—J. A. Fenwick, Captain; T. I. Lynch, G. B. Macrae, F. C. Worham, A. G. Fry, D. M. Spalding, B. Bogert, A. R. Pope, G. Miller, T. E. Tomlinson, A. Kerwin, Blair, D. Cameron, Russell, Cassells, D. G. Smythe and R. D. Radcliffe.

ST. NICHOLAS SKATING CLUB.—Thos. Barron, Captain; H. W. Slocum, R. D. Wrenn, Erskine Hewitt, E. A. Crowninshield, Malcolm Chace, W. A. Larned, J. W. Callender, C. M. Pope, Hobart, Livingston, Ward and G. M. Wharton.

SKATING CLUB OF BROOKLYN.—Howard Drakely, Captain; W. A. Barnett, J. A. Hall, Walker, McKenzie, Randall, 'Chaloner, Hallock, Wadsworth, Lehming, Wise and Hill.

CRESCENT ATHLETIC CLUB.—Carroll J. Post, Jr., Captain; Cavarly, Jewell, Garvin, Beaton, Miller, Roberts, C. H. Jacobs, Toerge, J. Lounsbury, Lever, Darrell and Curry.

The remaining members of the New York Hockey Club, undaunted by the desertion of their seven best men to the New York Athletic Club, got together one of the most clever teams that played ice hockey in the metropolitan district last winter. With headquarters still at the Ice Palace Rink, they played a series of sixteen matches, winning twelve, losing one and tieing three, as follows: Their one defeat was registered against them by their old members, the New York Athletic Club team, by a score of 4 to 1, but by grand work they tied this same team on two other occasions, the scores being 1 to 1 and 2 to 2. They met the St. Nicholas team twice, defeating them and playing a tie match of one goal each as well. Twice the Montclair Athletic Club lost to the New York Hockey Club by the close score of 1 to 0. The Skating Club of Brooklyn was defeated four times, the Crescent A. C. team three times, and Princeton University and Clifton (S. I.) Hockey Club one each. These men, all former Canadians, represented the club during the season: R. A. Hunt, Captain; O'Donnell, Leckie, Nelson, A. Knowlson, B. Phillips, de Casanova, Townsend and S. Phillips.

O'Donnell.   S. Phillips.   R. S. Hunt (Capt.)   Leckie.   Townsend.   B. Phillips.   de Casanova.

HOCKEY CLUB OF NEW YORK (FORMERLY NEW YORK HOCKEY CLUB), 1896–97.

Ranking next, by comparison of matches played, is the team of the Montclair (N. J.) Athletic Club. With no rink practice whatever, excepting that gained during their matches, this team played probably the most wonderful ice hockey of the winter, and many of the exhibitions in which they took part would have done credit to players of long experience. They defeated Yale University by 6 goals to 1, tied the St. Nicholas team on one occasion by a score of 3 goals each, lost to the champion New York A. C. team by the close score of 1 to 0, and by the same score, after a fierce struggle, lost to the All-Baltimore (Md.) team, a selected seven of the Baltimore Hockey League's best players. The complete record of their matches follows:

MONTCLAIR A. C. ICE HOCKEY TEAM RECORD—
SEASON OF 1896–97.

Date	Where Played		Goals		Goals
Dec. 5	...St. Nicholas Rink......	M. A. C.,	0	St. Nicholas Skating Club..	8
Dec. 11	..Ice Palace Rink........	"	0	New York Hockey Club....	1
Dec. 16	..Clermont Rink.........	"	6	Yale University...........	1
Dec. 29	..Clermont Rink.........	"	5	Crescent A. C.............	1
Jan. 5	....Clermont Rink.........	"	0	St. Nicholas Skating Club..	3
Jan. 15	..Ice Palace Rink........	"	0	New York Hockey Club ...	1
Jan. 16	...Montclair, N. J........	"	6	South Orange Field Club...	0
Jan. 21	...St. Nicholas Rink......	"	3	St. Nicholas Skating Club..	3
Jan. 26	..Clermont Rink........	"	1	Queen's University, Canada	6
Feb. 13	...Montclair, N. J........	"	7	Stevens Institute..........	2
Feb. 20	..St. Nicholas Rink......	"	2	St. Nicholas Skating Club..	6
Feb. 27	...Montclair, N. J........	"	12	Stevens Institute..........	3
Mch. 5	..Clermont Rink.........	"	3	Skating Club of Brooklyn..	0
Mch. 9	...St. Nicholas Rink......	"	0	New York A. C............	1
Mch. 13	..Baltimore (Md.) Rink..	"	0	All-Baltimore (Picked team)	1
Mch. 25	..Clermont Rink.........	"	4	Columbia University.......	1

The Montclair A. C. team was composed of the following players: Herman J. Koehler, Captain; M. R. Hornfeck, G. A. Hornfeck, H. F. Hornfeck, Allan N. Kennaday, Edwin J. Emerson, Arthur S. Williams, Lemuel Jacobus, Clarence Place and D. B. Mulligan.

Among other clubs who maintained representative ice hockey teams last winter are the Union Club, the Calumet Club, the St. Anthony Club and the Racquet and Tennis Club, who competed for a handsome ice hockey challenge cup presented by Mr. H. Percy Chubb. The Union Club team included

Homans.   Little.   Dickinson.   Henderson.   Wright.   Gunther.

Livingston (Capt.)   Delafield.

CUTLER SCHOOL (N. Y.) ICE HOCKEY TEAM.

Tied with Montclair High School for Championship of Inter-State Interscholastic Hockey League.

R. L. Stevens, E. Hewitt, G. Paddock, W. P. Coster, G. T. Warren, W. Nichols and S. Scheifflin, while the players of the Racquet and Tennis club team were P. Chubb, H. W. Slocum, H. Taylor, R. Stevens, H. Chubb, J. McClintock, S. de Garmendia, Grierson, Stoddard and Hewitt. The St. Anthony Club was represented by Littell, Hawley, Inman, Miles, Mortimer, Norrie and La Farge.

The Second and Third Divisions of the First Naval Battalion, State of New York, were represented by teams who played an interesting series of three matches, the Second Division winning all, with the following team : H. W. Walton, Captain ; J. D. O. Murray, E. Crawford, J. M. Mitchell, R. M. Crosby, R. Walden and D. B. Brigham. These men made up the team of the Third Division : Beebe, Captain ; Gilmore, Burtnett, Bill, Schirm, Achearn, Hunt, Folsome and Pentz.

The South Orange (N. J.) Field Club team played a number of creditable matches in the New York rinks, with the following men : R. Miles, Captain ; Jennings, Grulle, Conway, Allen, G. Miles, Watkins and L'Hommedieu. Another team, hailing from Orange, N. J., was that representing the Mountain Toboggan Club.

A team composed of members of the Orange Lake (N.Y.) Ice Yacht Club practiced and played a series of matches on their home ice, when weather permitted, with the Newburgh (N. Y.) Hockey Club, also appearing in the Clermont Rink on several occasions, and before the season was over played an excellent game. Their make-up included : C. M. Stebbins, Captain ; Trask, Chadwick, Gleich, E. A. Java, Leicht and H. J. Java.

Two good ice hockey teams were in existence on Staten Island last winter, viz., that representing the Staten Island Cricket and Base Ball Club and the Clifton Hockey Club. The latter included S. McDonnell, M. J. Kellion, J. B. Cornell, A. Thompson, W. Hardin, Jr., R. Manthrop, R. Lee, Jr., J. B. Lancaster, Keegan, O'Dwyer and Braniff.

Two companies of the Seventh Regiment, N. G. S. N. Y., were represented by teams who played several practice matches with outside teams, and they met on Feb. 23, at the St. Nicholas

J. D. O Murray. D. B. Brigham. L. Crawford. J. M. Mitchel. R. P. Walden.

H. W. Walton (Capt.) R. M. Crosby.

SECOND DIVISION, FIRST NAVAL BATTALION, S. N. Y., HOCKEY TEAM.

Rink, in a match for a trophy. The winning team was that of
the Tenth Company, who scored two goals to none by their
competitors, the Ninth Company. The players were as follows.

TENTH COMPANY.—Barron, Captain ; Spies, Scott, New-
combe, Hoy, La Farge and Maynard.

NINTH COMPANY.— Cavarly, Captain ; Coppell, Arthur,
Belden, Homans, Waring and Cragen.

◈

BOSTON.

Although Boston (Mass.), the home of ice polo, has no artificial-ice rink, they were quite fortunate last winter in being
favored with enough cold weather to give them quite steady
skating on their natural-ice rinks. The growth of ice hockey
in the States led to the adopting of the game by the Cambridge
(or sometimes called All-Massachusetts) Ice Polo and Hockey
Team, which put up a very fair article of ice hockey, defeating
a green Harvard University team and playing a close match
with the champion New York A. C. team, though they lost by
the score of 3 goals to none. They were the only team
from the States to make a Canadian tour last winter, and this
they very wrongfully did under the assumed title of a " Harvard
University " team. Six matches were played, and though all
were defeats, the Cambridge men learned much about ice
hockey, and consoled themselves with the fact that they were
not the only American team that had been accorded the self-
same reception in previous winters. The results of their
matches follow :

CAMBRIDGE ICE POLO AND HOCKEY TEAM RECORD—SEASON
OF 1896-97.

Date	Where Played	Goals		Goals
Feb. 3....Chute Rink Boston.....Cambridge,	4	Harvard University...	1
Feb. 5....Chutes Rink, Boston.....	"	5	Picked Team..........	0
Feb. 9.:..St. Nicholas Rink, N. Y..	"	1	St. Nicholas S. C......	2
Feb. 11...St. Nicholas Rink, N. Y..	"	0	New York A. C.......	3
Mch. 4...Victoria Rink, Montreal..	"	1	McGil University.....14
Mch. 6...Ottawa Rink............	"	2	Aberdeen H C.... ... 8
Mch. 8...Ottawa Rink............	"	3	Ottawa College.. 5
Mch. 9...Rideau Rink, Toronto...	"	0	All-Bank Team(picked) 7
Mch. 10..Kingston Rink..........	"	0	Frontenac H. C.......10
Mch. 11..Quebec Rink...........	"	3	Quebec H. C. (Senior). 8

S. Dodds. Cleveland. Kafer. C. Dodds. Childs.
Little. Roberts (Capt.) Brower.

LAWRENCEVILLE (N. J.) SCHOOL ICE HOCKEY TEAM, 1896-97.

The Cambridge team was composed entirely of New Englanders, some of whom are graduates of Massachusetts Institute of Technology, Brown University and Harvard   The captain was W. E. Jewell, Jr., and the other players were: "Jack" Corbett, of Harvard foot ball fame ; M. Lyman, H. A. Hopkins, Matteson, Lamb, H. Glidden, Morton, Burton and N. Tobey.

PITTSBURG.

The destruction by fire of the Schenley Park Casino of Pittsburg, on Dec. 17, 1896, put a damper on ice hockey in that city, from which there is no relief in sight as yet.   The game was highly popular, and excited so much interest during the winter of '95-'96 that two leagues were formed and schedules made ready (but necessarily never played) for the following winter. The teams entered in the Western Pennsylvania League were those representing the Pittsburg Hockey Club, Western University of Pennsylvania, Pittsburg Athletic Club and Duquesne Country and Athletic Club.   The second or Interscholastic League was composed of East Liberty Academy, Pittsburg High School, Pittsburg Academy, Pittsburg College, Shadyside Academy, and Duquesne College.   The Schenley Park Casino was the largest and without question the most beautiful artificial-ice skating rink ever constructed, being arranged with an immense stage and seating capacity for the accommodation of operatic productions during the summer season.   Ice hockey was first introduced to Pittsburg audiences by the visit of the Queens University team (senior champions of the Ontario Hockey Association), from Kingston, Canada, about two years ago, and a series of friendly matches between the Montreal and Shamrock teams, both of Montreal, during the same season.

CHICAGO.

An artificial-ice rink was maintained in " Tattersalls " big auditorium in Chicago, and much ice hockey was played there during the winter '95-'96, and although the sport appeared to be gaining in popularity, this rink was not opened last winter.

The Chicago Athletic Association was the principal exponent
of the game, their matches with a visiting aggregation of
Canadians called "Spalding's Team," proving of great
interest. This same team traveled to Minneapolis, St. Paul,
Milwaukee, Detroit and Buffalo, in all of which cities natural-
ice rinks flourish and ice hockey is played more or less and is
rapidly growing in favor.

BALTIMORE.

Baltimore is probably the most enthusiastic ice hockey city
in the country. Soon after the sport was introduced to the
States the Baltimoreans took it up with great earnestness and
an artificial-ice rink, the North Avenue Ice Palace, was
opened in Baltimore about three years ago. Since then this
rink has furnished an arena for many fierce and exciting
matches and the large audiences which turn out for every
scheduled game, show a most generous appreciation of the
sport. This intense interest may be partly accounted for by
the fact that in the South it is practically impossible to enjoy
ice sports on any but artificial-ice, and the climate is too mild
to supply natural-ice for the purpose.

A keen rivalry existed between the teams representing Johns
Hopkins University and the Baltimore Athletic Club the first
season that the rink was opened. Dr. W. A. Bisnaw, familiarly
known as "the father of Baltimore's hockey" and Mr. S. Alf.
Mitchell, formerly of Queens University Hockey Team, of
Kingston, Canada, who was studying in Baltimore, did much
to promote and develop the players of these teams, and under
their able coaching they soon became quite as expert as their
rivals in more northern cities. Later the Baltimore Hockey
Club was organized and included C. K. Harrison, Jr., Captain ;
Harry E. Perry T. B. Harrison, Milton Whitehurst, G. Reese,
H. Haughton, Harry Jenkins, Charles F. Corning, and E.
Parmly, Jr. This was a very formidable aggregation, being
the pick of Baltimore's best men at the game. The club disbanded about January 15th, 1897, to assist in forming an ice
hockey league.

During January, 1897, the Baltimore Hockey League was organized, and the fierce struggle which ensued for the possession of the championship trophy, the Northampton Cup, presented by Mr. J. S. Filon, is probably without precedent. Four teams composed the league, as follows: Maryland Athletic Club, University of Maryland, Johns Hopkins University, and Northampton Hockey Club. A series of six matches was arranged for each team, which was to meet each opponent in two matches, all to be played at the North Avenue Ice Palace Rink, between February 2d and March 26th. The completion of the regular scheduled matches found two teams tied for first honors with five wins and one loss each, and the other two tied for third place. Two extra matches were played to decide these ties, with the following result:

BALTIMORE HOCKEY LEAGUE—SEASON OF 1896-97.

SUMMARY BY MATCHES.

	Won	Lost	Tied
Maryland Athletic Club	6	1	1
*University of Maryland	5	2	0
Northampton Hockey Club	2	5	0
Johns Hopkins University	1	6	1

*Declared champions by decision of court (see below).

Unfortunately, however, the championship was far from determined as future developments proved. The final contest between the leaders had awakened intense interest throughout the city and was a very close match. After a most severe and very rough struggle the Maryland Athletic Club team earned two goals to one secured by the University, and were conceded the winners by almost everyone in the immense audience, when just before the final call of time in the second half the University of Maryland was awarded a goal which tied the score, by Umpire Walter Whitehurst. As the shot was a high one and questioned by many, a long dispute followed. The specified time having expired, the referee, G. B. Macrae of the New York Athletic Club, ordered the match to continue, and (under the rules*) as the University of Maryland scored the

*Rules of the Amateur Hockey Association of Canada were adopted by the Baltimore Hockey League.

first goal during the play-off they were declared the winners of
the match by 3 goals to 2.

Immediately the play was finished a protest of the umpire's
decision was entered by the Maryland Athletic Club, claiming
the disputed goal was no goal, and with it thrown out the score
at the end of the match would have been 2 to 1 in their favor.
The protest was heard by the executive committee of the
league, who took much evidence as to whether or not the goal
was fairly shot. On vote of this committee it was decided that
the goal was not shot, and that the Maryland Athletic Club
was entitled to the match, championship title and Northampton
cup, the latter being promptly turned over to their custody.

This awoke the greatest indignation among the University of
Maryland students, who declared from the first that under the
rules governing the play it was illegal to change the umpire's
decision.   Considerable bitter feeling was engendered, which
grew to such extent that the University men took the matter
into court and replevined the cup, but the Athletic Club
stolidly refused to relinquish their hold upon it.

This made the affair still deeper in the mire, and on Sept.
30th, 1897, the University of Maryland retained three prominent lawyers and brought suit against the Athletic Club to
obtain possession of the much-coveted and disputed cup.
Justice Bailey, who heard the petition which involved the
point as to whether or not an umpire's decision in an ice
hockey game is final, after listening to many witnesses from
both sides, decided, on Oct. 16th, that according to the rules
played under, there was no appeal from the umpire's decision
on the question of goals, and that by the decision of the
umpire the match in question and likewise the championship
was won by the University of Maryland.   The cup was also
ordered turned over to the rightful holders.   This gives the
University one leg on the cup, which must be won three different seasons before becoming the property of any league
member.

According to the above decision the corrected and final
standing of the teams was :

SUMMARY BY MATCHES.

	Won	Lost	Tied
University of Maryland..................................	6	1	1
Maryland Athletic Club.................................	5	2	0
Northampton Hockey Club	2	5	0
Johns Hopkins University	1	6	1

UNIVERSITY OF MARYLAND ICE HOCKEY TEAM—RECORD OF
LEAGUE MATCHES, SEASON OF 1896–97.

Date	Where Played	Goals		Goals
Feb. 2,	North Ave. Ice Palace, U. of M.,	1	Maryland A. C................	2
Feb. 5,	" " "	3	Johns Hopkins Univ.........	1
Feb. 12,	" " "	6	Northampton H. C...........	0
Feb. 26,	" " "	1	Maryland A. C.........	0
Mch. 12,	" " "	0	Johns Hopkins Univ.........	0
Mch. 19,	" " "	2	Northampton H. C...........	1
Mch. 20,	" " "	4	Johns Hopkins Univ......'.....	0
Mch. 23,	" " "	3	Maryland A. C................	2

The match of March 12 lasted one hour and forty minutes,
actual playing time, without either side scoring. As the
players were so fatigued they could hardly skate, the match
was called and played off on March 20th.

The personnel of the teams comprising the Baltimore Hockey
League follows :

UNIVERSITY OF MARYLAND—M. Whitehurst, Captain ; W.
R. Pond, E. A. Charbonnel, Albert Baker, Henry Kennard,
S. Deal, H. Whitehurst, Geo. Hicks, F. Weller and H. A.
Cotton.

MARYLAND ATHLETIC CLUB—Peterson, Captain ; H. E.
Perry, W. F. Duffy, Focke, Simmonds, C. Corning, Cochran,
Krebs, C. Harrison and A. Corning.

NORTHAMPTON HOCKEY CLUB—Dr. W. A. Bisnaw, Captain ;
H. J. C. Ritchie, W. C. McCullough, Gordon Reese, B. Wagner,
L. McCabe, P. Goodwin, Smallwood, C. German, Meyers, Mc-
Cormick, Houston, Green, Flemming, F. C. Porter and I.
Owings.

JOHNS HOPKINS UNIVERSITY—A. F. Mitchell, Captain ;
Williams, Hodges, Denmead, Hillis, Hill, Scholl, Hall, Naylor,
Nelson, Leary and Bagg.

The following exhibition matches were played by the Baltimore Hockey Club, before it disbanded, and the several teams
of the Baltimore Hockey League during the season. It is well

to state in this connection that the Baltimore rink, the North Avenue Ice Palace, is scarcely thirty feet in width, so narrow in fact that the home teams have adopted a formation, seen no where else. They play but three forwards on their line and instead of abolishing the fourth forward (whom they should drop entirely, as there is no room for him), he plays behind the line and is known as "rover." This fact prevents any fair comparison of play by Northern teams on this ice, the narrow surface destroying their team-work by not permitting them to play their forwards in their usual positions.

SOME PROMINENT EXHIBITION MATCHES PLAYED BY THE BALTIMORE TEAMS DURING THE SEASON OF 1896-97.

Date		Goals		Goals
Dec. 16	Baltimore Hockey Club	3	Johns Hopkins University	0
Dec. 23	Baltimore Hockey Club	3	Maryland A. C.	3
Dec. 30	Johns Hopkins University	4	Maryland A. C.	2
Jan. 8	Johns Hopkins University	2	Yale University	2
Jan. 9	Baltimore Hockey Club	0	Yale University	3
Feb. 13	Maryland A. C.	4	Princeton University	1
*Feb. 19	University of Maryland	2	University of Pennsylvania	2
Feb. 20	Johns Hopkins University	3	University of Pennsylvania	2
Feb. 27	Maryland A. C.	0	St. Nicholas S. C.	1
March 6	University of Maryland	0	New York A. C.	5
March 9	All-Baltimore (picked team)	3	Montreal H. C. (Senior)	5
March 10	All-Baltimore " "	0	Shamrock H. C. (Senior)	3
March 13	All-Baltimore " "	1	Montclair A. C.	0

*Forfeited to U. of P.

WASHINGTON.

Though a splendid artificial-ice rink has been in existence in Washington, D. C., for a couple of years, ice hockey has not met with favor, and for some unknown reason does not thrive as in all other localities wherever the game has been introduced. The Washington Hockey Club is still in existence and has played a number of inter-city matches with different Baltimore teams, but in most instances has lost.

ICE HOCKEY IN THE COLLEGES AND SCHOOLS.

To Yale University belongs the credit for the importation of ice hockey into the States, or more correctly, to the efforts of Malcolm G. Chace and Arthur E. Foote, of Yale. These men, who are both lawn tennis experts, learned of the popularity and fascination of ice hockey while on one of their visits to Canadian tennis tournaments, and both became confirmed devotees of the sport at first sight. The following winter (about 1894) this pair organized a team of Yale skaters, most of whom were tennis cracks, and during the Christmas holidays a tour of the prominent Canadian rinks was made.

Of course the American players (who had previously practiced with only a rubber ball instead of a puck) were sadly defeated in all the matches they undertook, but the trip was regarded as a success, as it furnished much excellent sport, the best sort of instruction, and created no end of enthusiasm in the breasts of the visitors. They all praised the game highly upon their return, and went at it with renewed vigor each season, and from this introduction it has rapidly spread to its present popularity.

Yale's first public match of any importance in this country was played in the St. Nicholas rink in New York on April 1, 1896. It was against the St. Nicholas Skating Club team, who were favored with artificial-ice for steady, daily practice, while the college team was necessarily dependent upon varying conditions of natural-ice, or more often none at all. The St. Nicholas team won by five goals to one, the teams lining up as follows :

St. Nicholas S. C.	Positions	Yale University
T. Barron		H. Rider
W. A. Larned		J. Hall
R. L. Stevens	......Forwards......	M. G. Chace, Capt.
E. A. Crowninshield		A. Barnes
Anderson, Capt............Cover Point.. .		C. S. Morris
R. D. Wrenn..................Point...........W. Corbin		
H. W. Slocum.................Goal............W. Barnett		

Cornell University was the next to take up the game, and appeared in a match with the St. Nicholas team, at the latter's rink, on March 28, 1896, losing by a score of eight goals to none. The Cornell team included H. H. Lyle, Captain ; Stevens, J. C. Nellegar and C. R. Wyckoff, forwards ; A. Meiklejohn, cover point ; H. H. Milbourn, point, and R. C. Mysenburg, goal.

With a few changes this team played a number of matches last winter, and the sport has every indication of becoming a permanent one at Cornell.

Yale played by far the best game among the college teams last winter, notable in her schedule being the match played with Queens University of Kingston, Canada, champions of the Ontario Hockey Association for the past two years. A complete schedule follows :

Yale University Ice Hockey Team Record— Season of 1896–97.

Date		Goals		Goals
Dec. 16...Clermont Rink.........Yale Univ.,	1		Montclair A. C..........	6
Dec. 24...St. Nicholas Rink...... "	2		St. Nicholas S. C........	3
Jan. 8....Baltimore (Md.) Rink.. "	2		Johns Hopkins Univ....	2
Jan. 9....Baltimore (Md.) Rink.. "	3		Baltimore Hockey Club..	0
Jan. 13...St Nicholas Rink...... "	1		New York A. C.........	?
Jan. 23...St. Nicholas Rink...... "	0		Queens Univ. of Canada,	3
Feb. 13...St. Nicholas Rink...... "	0		New York A. C..........	5
Mch. 13..St. Nicholas Rink...... "	1		St. Nicholas S. C........	3
Mch. 27..St. Nicholas Rink...... "	7		Columbia University....	2

The players who represented Yale last winter included : A. F. Barnes, '97, Captain ; G. P. Sheldon, Jr., '99; H. V. Ryder, '97 ; J. A. Hall, '97 ; C. S. Morris, '97 ; S. S. Stoddard, '99 ; H. Sutton, '97 ; W. A. Barnett, '98 ; H. Morris, H. C. Smith, C. Walworth and Fincke.

The excellent work done by the University of Maryland team and that which represented Johns Hopkins University of

Baltimore, has been covered by description on page 37. These teams rank in the order mentioned next to Yale, and quite possibly would have defeated Yale had they met in competition.

Princeton University had a team in the field last winter, composed of the following men : Robb, Poe, Evans, Hillebrand, Ayers, Pardee, Wheeler, Brokaw, Daniels, Stevenson, Atland, Holt, Spurgin, and Blair. This not being an authorized 'varsity organization, some objection was raised by those in authority at Princeton and the team thus prevented from playing a number of scheduled matches. These games were played :

PRINCETON UNIVERSITY ICE HOCKEY TEAM RECORD—SEASON OF 1896-97.

Date	Where Played	Goals		Goals
Jan. 15..Clermont Rink.........	Princeton Univ.,	0	S. C. of Brooklyn...	3
Feb. 10..Ice Palace Rink........	"	0	N. Y. Hockey Club.	2
Feb. 11..Clermont Rink.........	"	2	S. C. of Brooklyn...	0
Feb. 13..Baltimore (Md.) Rink..	"	1	Maryland A. C......	4

University of Pennsylvania's ice hockey team labored under the same disadvantages as Yale and Princeton as regards natural-ice only for practice. They put up several stiff matches however, and should improve in team work—their weakness—this winter, as Philadelphia is to have a fine artificial-ice rink. The results of their games follow :

UNIVERSITY OF PENNSYLVANIA ICE HOCKEY TEAM RECORD—SEASON OF 1896-97.

Date	Where Played	Goals		Goals
*Feb. 19....Baltimore (Md.) Rink....	U. of P.,	2	Univ. of Maryland....	2
Feb. 20....Baltimore (Md.) Rink....	"	2	Johns Hopkins Univ..	3
Feb. 26....St. Nicholas Rink........	"	5	Columbia University..	0

*Forfeited to U. of P.

These men made up the team : S. Willet, Agnew, Phymister, G. W. Orton, H. J. Gibbons, Rogers, Stanley, Mechling, Decker, Laird, Smith, Jarvis, Moore, Chattin, Gosman, Stackhouse and Falke. The first four are Canadians and splendid hockey players, particularly Agnew, whose work in the match against Columbia was marvelous.

Columbia University's team showed little improvement throughout the season, though being located within a short

distance of the metropolitan rinks, where they secured abund-
ant practice compared to most of their competitors. The personnel of the team was: Van Voorhis, Captain; Tilt, Mortimer,.
Belden, Roberts, O'Dwyer, Longacre, Williams, Putnam, Hall,
Pell, Elliott and O'Conner, and their record of matches follows:

COLUMBIA UNIVERSITY ICE HOCKEY TEAM RECORD—SEASON
OF 1896-97.

Date	Where Played		Goals		Goals
Jan. 8....	Clermont Rink.....	Columbia Univ.,	0	S. C. of Brooklyn......	0
Feb. 15...	Ice Palace Rink....	"	" 4	3d Div., 1st Naval Bat.	1
Feb. 26...	St. Nicholas Rink..	"	" 0	Univ. of Pennsylvania.	5
Mch. 25	Clermont Rink	"	" 1	Montclair A. C.........	5
Mch. 27..	St. Nicholas Rink..	"	" 2	Yale University........	7

Harvard University only attempted ice hockey late last
winter and played but few matches, their attention having been
previously devoted to ice polo entirely. These men were on
the hockey team : Goodridge, Beardsell, Stevens, Clark, Bald-
win, Dunlop and Elliot.

Stevens Institute of Hoboken, N. J., was represented by the
following team last winter, which made a very creditable show-
ing in a number of matches, considering the little practice ob-
tainable : J. Brune, Captain; Grady, W. Chapin, Scott, Sanson,
Christy, Frank, J. C. Palmer, E. E. Palmer, Kennedy and
Grelle. Their best exhibition was that of March 30th, at the
St. Nicholas Rink, where they defeated the Third Division,
First Naval Battalion, by a score of 1–0.

Rutgers College supported an ice hockey team with this
personnel : Mills, Captain ; Stryker, Carbon, Drury, Scudder,
Barrett and Van Clef.

Some excellent exhibition matches were played by the schools
of the Metropolitan district last winter, and near the close of
the season the rivalry thus aroused led to the formation of the
Interstate Interscholastic Ice Hockey League, with the following members: Montclair (N. J) High School, St. Austin's
School of Staten Island, and Cutler, De La Salle and Berkeley
Schools of New York City. Two silver cups were purchased
to be awarded the teams finishing first and second in a series of
matches, which resulted as follows :

INTERSTATE INTERSCHOLASTIC ICE HOCKEY LEAGUE--RECORD
OF MATCHES—SEASON OF 1897.

Date	Where Played		Goals		Goals
March 13....	St. Nicholas Rink......	De La Salle.....	2	St. Austin's.......	0
March 16....	St. Nicholas Rink......	Montclair.......	7	Berkeley	0
March 17....	Clermont Rink.........	St. Austin's.....	3	Berkeley	3
March 18....	St. Nicholas Rink......	Cutler..........	7	De La Salle.......	3
March 20....	St. Nicholas Rink......	Cutler..........	9	Berkeley	0
March 23....	Clermont Rink........	Montclair.......	5	De La Salle.......	0
March 24....	Clermont Rink........	Cutler..........	3	St. Austin's.......	0
March 25....	St. Nicholas Rink......	Montclair.......	2	Cutler............	2
March 26....	Clermont Rink..... ...	Montclair.......	5	St. Austin's.......	1
April 1.....	St. Nicholas Rink......	De La Salle.....	1	Berkeley	1

SUMMARY BY MATCHES.	Won	Lost	Tied
Montclair High School.........................	3	0	1
Cutler School...	3	0	1
De La Salle School......................................	1	2	1
Berkeley School..	0	2	2
St. Austin's School......................................	0	3	1

SUMMARY BY GOALS.	Scored	Opponents Scored
Montclair High School.............................	19	3
Cutler School....................................	21	5
De La Salle School...............................	6	13
Berkeley School..................................	4	20
St. Austin's School...............................	4	13

As the record of matches indicates, the championship was
not decided, and at this writing the matter still hangs fire.
Much comment was caused by the tie match of March 25th,
between the two leaders in the race, which if decided, would
have determined the champions, and winner of the cup for
second place as well. One of the goal decisions against Montclair in this match was questioned by all who saw it save the
umpire, the puck being stopped by the Cutler goal-tend's
skates while standing very plainly behind the goal line. Montclair protested, but to no avail, and as developments proved,
this goal, if allowed, would have won the match for them by a
score of 3 to 2. Many disinterested witnesses also claimed
that final time should have been called some moments before
Cutler scored their last goal which tied the score.

The referee, Mr. R. Paulding, of Berkeley School, also
president of the Interscholastic League, appointed March 31st,
at the Clermont Rink, for the play-off of the tie. The Cutler
team refused to appear at the time set and Montclair should
have been awarded the championship by default, but certain
wire-pulling caused either a tie vote or prevented a quorum

being present at any of the numerous meetings called for the settlement of the affair at the request of the Montclair delegates.

The personnel of the teams composing the Interstate Interscholastic Ice Hockey League last season was as follows :

MONTCLAIR HIGH SCHOOL—Gustave A. Hornfeck, Captain; A. Griffen, Chas. Phillips, Al. Lindley, W. McBurney, C. Anderson, Edward Cary and Reginald Trautschold.

CUTLER SCHOOL—Livingston, Captain ; Homans, Little, Dickinson, Henderson, Wright, Delafield, Gunther and Inman.

DE LA SALLE SCHOOL—McCabe, Brennan, O'Byrne, Dwyer, Robbins, Corrigan and Tilford.

BERKELEY SCHOOL—Paulding, Captain; Arthur, Rice, Pell, Bien, Gulden, Procter, Huntington, Thomas and Granberry.

ST. AUSTIN'S SCHOOL—Scofield, V. Scott, B. Scott, Wall, Lindsay, Heineken, Bonner, Taylor, Pope, Thomas, Dearborn and Lawrence.

Another young team which made an enviable ice hockey record was that representing Lawrenceville School of Lawrenceville, N. J. Though their competition was confined to three outside matches, the results stand as good vouchers of their ability to cope with any school team in the country. Their record follows :

LAWRENCEVILLE SCHOOL ICE HOCKEY TEAM RECORD—SEASON
OF 1896-97.

Date	Where Played		Goals		Goals
Jan. 13	Lawrenceville, N. J.	L'ville Sch.,	2	Princeton Univ. (scrub)	0
Feb. 16	Lawrenceville, N. J.	" "	8	Rutgers College	0
Mch. 6	St. Nicholas Rink, N. Y.	" "	2	Cutler School	1

These players made up the Lawrenceville School team : Roberts, Captain ; Cleveland, C. Dodds, S. Dodds, Kafer, Little, Brower and Childs.

Columbia Grammar School of New York and St. Paul's School of Long Island played several good ice hockey matches during the winter, and should have been members of the Interstate Interscholastic Ice Hockey League. The latter's players were as follows : Cooke, Beyers, Coxe, Hunterson, Levey, Alexander and Illingworth.

CANADIAN ICE HOCKEY.

Throughout Canada ice hockey is as common as base ball in the States. Nearly every town, social club, college and school has its representative team, and many banks and business houses are represented as well. Dozens of leagues have been organized for years, and each winter they promote series of competitions which keep the sport booming.

Many towns and cities in Canada have a "Victoria" hockey club, the name being so commonly popular and adopted by so many different clubs that it is necessary to mention their locality in order to distinguish one from the other.

The larger leagues and associations offer trophies for competition to junior and intermediate teams as well as to the senior teams representing the clubs or organizations composing the body. This is done to develop the young players, and the scheme works to perfection. No club is allowed to compete for the senior championship until it has won the intermediate championship, and likewise a club must first win the junior series before being eligible to compete with the intermediates. Also, no man may play in the intermediate series who has taken part in more than one senior match in the same season, and no man is eligible to play in the junior series who has played in more than one intermediate match or in any senior match during the same season.

AMATEUR HOCKEY ASSOCIATION OF CANADA.

The most prominent league in existence is the Amateur Hockey Association of Canada, composed of these clubs: Victoria Hockey Club of Montreal, Ottawa Hockey Club, Montreal Hockey Club, Quebec Hockey Club and Shamrock Hockey Club of Montreal.

COLUMBIA UNIVERSITY ICE HOCKEY TEAM.

The Montreal Hockey Club won the championship of the Amateur Hockey Association of Canada in 1888, and held it for eight consecutive years, when the Victoria Club wrested the coveted title from them.

The Victorias of Montreal are the present champions of their association, and also hold the Stanley Cup, emblematic of the ice hockey championship of the world. The clubs of this Association play a series of home matches between January 1st and March 8th of each year, the winner of the most matches being declared the champions. The senior series of 1897 resulted as follows:

AMATEUR HOCKEY ASSOCIATION OF CANADA—RECORD OF SENIOR MATCHES—SEASON OF 1897.

	Victoria	Ottawa	Montreal	Quebec	Shamrock	VICTORIES
Victoria......................	..	1	2	2	2	7
Ottawa......................	1	..	1	2	2	6
Montreal.....................	0	1	..	2	2	5
Quebec.......................	0	0	0	..	1	1
Shamrock.....................	0	0	0	1	..	1
DEFEATS......................	1	2	3	7	7	

From this it will be seen that the Victoria team lost but one match, that being to Ottawa. The champion team was made up as follows: M. Grant, Captain ; Robert Macdougall, Hortland Macdougall, Robert Lewis, Shirley Davidson, Harold Henderson, Ernest McLea, Drinkwater, H. Molson and David Gillellan.

A. II. A. OF C.—INTERMEDIATE SERIES.

In the 1897 series for the intermediate championship of this league five teams competed—from the same clubs composing the senior series. The result was a tie for first place between the Montreal and Shamrock clubs. The first match played to decide the tie resulted in an even score, but the second proved Montreal the intermediate champions.

T. Barrow.   J. W. Callender.   E. A. Crowninshield.   H. W. Slocum.
C. M. Pope.   R. D. Wrenn.
Erskine Hewitt.   W. A. Larned.

ST. NICHOLAS SKATING CLUB HOCKEY TEAM, 1896-97.

The senior teams of the Montreal and Shamrock clubs made a tour through the States last winter and played the following exhibition matches:

Date	Where Played	Goals		Goals
Mch. 8..	Balto. (Md.) Rink..Montreal H. C..	4	Shamrock H. C........	4
Mch. 9..	" " ..Montreal H. C..	8	Shamrock H. C	3
Mch. 9..	" " ..Montreal H. C .	5	All-Balto. (picked team)	3
Mch. 10..	" " ..Montreal H. C..	3	Shamrock H. C........	2
Mch. 10..	" " ..Shamrock H. C.	3	All-Balto. (picked team)	0
Mch. 11..	Clermont Rink....Montreal H. C..	3	Shamrock H. C........	2
Mch. 13..	" " ....Shamrock H. C.	3	Montreal H. C........	1

The Montreal team included: H. C. Collins, Wm. Murphy, M. Grant, N. Dawes, A. Hough, D. Gillellan and H. Baird. R. Wall, L. Belcourt, J. Stephens, W. Dobby, D. Brown, Doblitz, C. Farrell and Pagnuelo composed the Shamrocks.

MANITOBA AND NORTHWEST AMATEUR HOCKEY ASSOCIATION.

As regards playing strength and prominence the Manitoba and Northwest Amateur Hockey Association of Winnipeg ranks second, though the wonderful skill displayed by their champion Victoria team is probably on a par with that of the Victorias of Montreal. This fact was proven when these teams met in competition for the Stanley Cup and championship of the world.

But two clubs entered the senior competition in this association last winter, the Victoria Hockey Club of Winnipeg, who have held the championship of their association for the past six years, and the Winnipeg Hockey Club, the former club winning four of a series of five matches played, as follows:

MANITOBA AND NORTHWEST AMATEUR HOCKEY ASSOCIATION
—RECORD OF SENIOR MATCHES—SEASON OF 1896–97.

	Goals			Goals
Victoria Hockey Club............	3	Winnipeg Hockey Club..........	2
" "	3	" "	0
" "	7	" "	4
" "	6	" "	7
" "	4	" "	3

The players making up the champion Victoria team were as follows: Armytage, Captain ; Bain, Campbell, Howard, Johnston, Flett and Merritt.

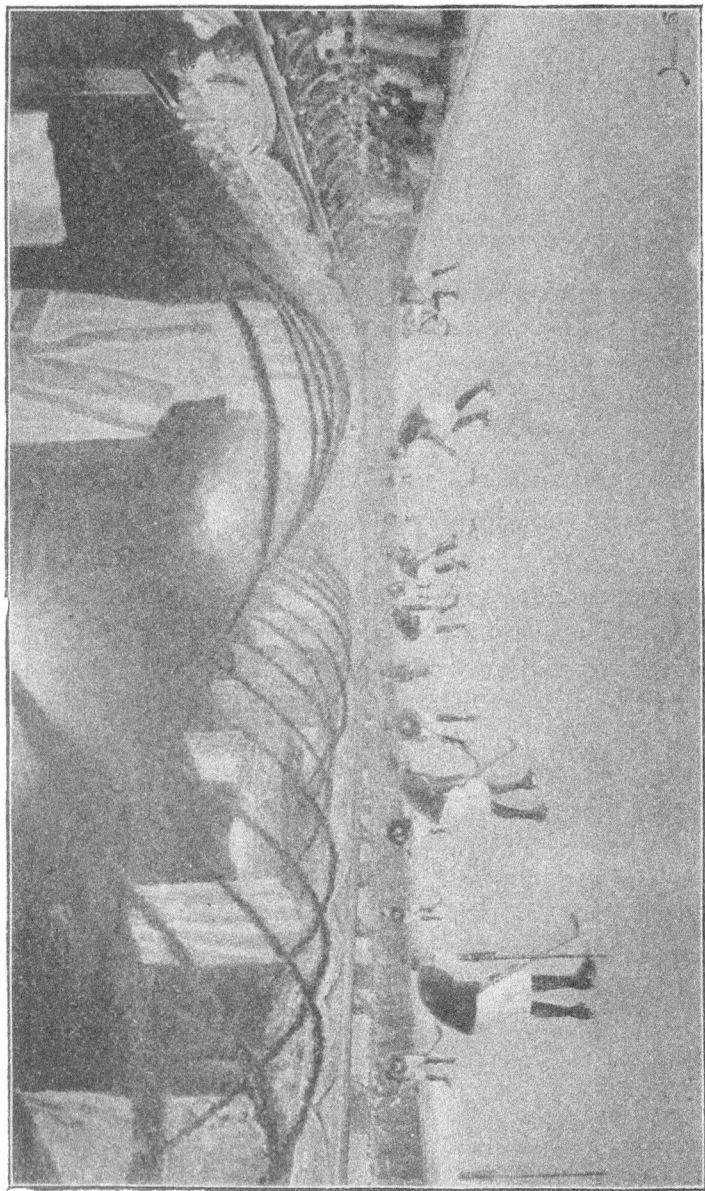

MONTREALS vs. VICTORIAS, AT THE VICTORIA RINK, MONTREAL, JANUARY, 1897.

A CHAMPIONSHIP MATCH IN THE SENIOR SERIES OF THE AMATEUR HOCKEY LEAGUE OF CANADA.

M. AND N. A. H. A.—INTERMEDIATE SERIES.

Four clubs composed the intermediate series last winter, viz., Winnipeg Hockey Club, Victoria Hockey Club of Winnipeg, Portage la Prairie Hockey Club and St. Johns Hockey Club. Their home-and-home matches resulted as follows :

MANITOBA AND NORTHWEST AMATEUR HOCKEY ASSOCIATION
—RECORD OF INTERMEDIATE MATCHES—SEASON OF '96-97.

	Goals		Goals
Victoria H. C.	3	Winnipeg H. C.	2
Portage la Prairie H. C.	7	St. Johns H. C.	6
Winnipeg H. C.	3	Portage la Prairie H. C.	2
Victoria H. C.	5	St. Johns H. C.	0
Winnipeg H. C.	8	St. Johns H. C.	2
Victoria H. C.	7	St. Johns H. C.	6
Portage la Prairie H. C.	5	Victoria H. C.	4
Winnipeg H. C.	5	Victoria H. C.	4
Portage la Prairie H. C.	6	St. Johns H. C.	3
Portage la Prairie H. C.	5	Winnipeg H. C.	4
Winnipeg H. C.	7	St. Johns H. C.	3
Victoria H. C.	4	Portage la Prairie H. C.	2

SUMMARY BY MATCHES.

	Won	Lost
Winnipeg H. C.	4	2
Victoria H. C.	4	2
Portage la Prairie H. C.	4	2
St. Johns H. C.	0	6

SUMMARY BY GOALS.

	Scored	Opponents Scored
Winnipeg H. C.	29	19
Victoria H. C.	27	20
Portage la Prairie H. C.	27	24
St. Johns H. C.	20	40

ONTARIO HOCKEY ASSOCIATION.

The third league in importance in Canadian hockey circles is the Ontario Hockey Association, which is centered about Toronto. The members of this body compete annually (during the months of January and February), by *tie* matches, for the possession of the Crosby Challenge Cup.

The *tie* matches, which are arranged under the direction of the Executive, are simply the pairing off of the several teams entered, exactly as the entries for a lawn tennis tournament in this country are drawn, for the preliminary or first round of play. Home-and-home matches are played to decide each tie, and a majority of the goals scored in both matches determines the winner of the tie. The winners of the first round play off their ties, and so on until one club or team wins the final tie and championship.

This method was adopted by this league because its members were so widely scattered, and much expense and traveling is thus saved. These tie matches are arranged openly (not drawn at random from a blind pool), and neighboring teams are usually paired together. The list of competitors in the final ties and the champions for the last seven years in this league is as follows :

CHAMPIONS OF THE ONTARIO HOCKEY ASSOCIATION—

SENIOR SERIES.

Goals

1891....Ottawa H. C.............	defeated	Queens University........	4 to 1
1892....Ottawa H. C.............	"	Osgoode Hall............	10 to 4
1893....Ottawa H. C.............	"	Queens University	6 to 3
1894 .. Osgoode Hall............	"	Queens University	3 to 2
1895 . Queens University.......	"	Trinity University.......	17 to 3
1896....Queens University.......	"	Stratford H. C...........	12 to 3
1897....Queens University.......	"	Toronto University......	12 to 7

The senior series of 1897 resulted as follows :

ONTARIO HOCKEY ASSOCIATION—RECORD OF SENIOR

MATCHES—SEASON OF 1897.

FIRST ROUND.   Goals

Toronto University.............defeated Stratford H. C........... 9 to 2
Stratford H. C..................   ",   Toronto University...... 4 to 2

     Toronto University wins ....11 to 6

Toronto A. C........ ......defeated Trinity University....... 6 to 4
Toronto A. C.................. "   Trinity University....... 3 to 2

     Toronto A. C. wins.. 9 to 6

Toronto A. C...................defeated Osgoode Hall............ 7 to 1
Osgoode Hall................ .... "   Toronto A. C............ 4 to 2

     Toronto A. C wins.. 9 to 5

Peterboro H. C..................defeated Royal Military College... 8 to 3
Peterboro H. C................ "   Royal Military College... 3 to 0

     Peterboro H. C. wins..11 to 3

SECOND ROUND.

Toronto University.............defeated Toronto A. C............ 2 to 0
Toronto University............. " Toronto A. C............ 5 to 1

Toronto University wins............................... 7 to 1

Queens University. ....defeated Peterboro H. C........... 6 to 4
Queens University............. " Peterboro H. C.......by default

Queens University wins..... .... 6 to 4

FINAL ROUND.

Queens University.............defeated Toronto University...... 6 to 1
Queens University............. tied Toronto University...... 6 to 6

Queens University wins Senior Championship.................12 to 7

As shown above, the famous Queens University team of
Kingston, Ontario, again turned up winners of the senior
championship, a title which they have now held for the past
three years, or ever since they have played under the very
capable generalship of Dr. J. J. Harty, one of the most able
hockeyists ever produced by Canada.   This famous captain is
residing in New York City this winter, and will undoubtedly
be seen as a member of the St. Nicholas Skating Club's hockey
team during the season.   Previous to becoming champions of
their league in 1895, the Queens University team figured in
the final tie match three out of four consecutive seasons.

The personnel of the championship team of 1897 was as follows: Dr. J. J. Harty, Captain; Guy Curtis, Merrill, Dalton,
Hiscock, Weatherhead and Brock.

This team, with the addition of two graduates, Cunningham
and Waldron, made a tour to New York and Brooklyn last
winter and figured in the following exhibition matches:

Date.	Where Played.		Goals.		Goals.
Jan. 23	St. Nicholas Rink	Queens University	3	Yale University.	0
Jan. 25	St. Nicholas Rink	"	1	St. Nicholas S. C.	1
Jan. 26	Clermont Rink	"	6	Montclair A. C.	1

O. H. A.—INTERMEDIATE SERIES.

For the intermediate honors of the Ontario Hockey Association last season fifteen teams competed, the Berlin Hockey
Club winning after a long struggle.   The ties and winners
were as follows:

ONTARIO HOCKEY ASSOCIATION—RECORD OF INTERMEDIATE MATCHES—SEASON OF 1897.

FIRST ROUND.

Toronto A. C. defeated Osgoode Hall; Victoria H. C. of Toronto defeated Osgoode Hall (by default); Victoria H. C. of Toronto defeated Toronto A. C. Victoria H. C. winners of tie.

Brampton H. C. defeated Ayr H C.; Berlin H. C. defeated Ayr H. C.; Berlin H. C. defeated Brampton H. C. Berlin H. C. winners of tie.

Orillia H. C. defeated Collingwood H. C.; Barrie H. C defeated Orillia H. C. Barrie H. C. winners of tie.

Sarina H. C. defeated Petrolia H. C.; London H. C. defeated Petrolia H. C.; London H. C. defeated Sarina H. C. London H. C. winners of tie.

Peterboro H. C. defeated Norwood H. C.; Frontenac H. C. defeated Peterboro H. C. Frontenac H. C. winners of tie.

SECOND ROUND.

Berlin H. C. defeated London H. C.; Berlin H. C. defeated Barrie H. C. Berlin H. C. winners of tie.

Frontenac H. C. defeated Victoria H. C. of Toronto (by default).

FINAL ROUND.

Berlin H. C. defeated Frontenac H. C., 3 to 0. Berlin H. C. winning Intermediate Championship.

O. H. A.—JUNIOR SERIES.

Nineteen teams entered the Junior series, with results as follows:

ONTARIO HOCKEY ASSOCIATION—RECORD OF JUNIOR MATCHES—SEASON OF 1897.

FIRST ROUND.

Peterboro H. C. defeated Norwood H. C., 8 to 3; Norwood H. C. defeated Peterboro H. C., 4 to 2. Peterboro H. C. winners of tie, 10 to 7.

Frontenac H. C. defeated Queens University. Frontenac H. C. winners of tie.

Wellington H. C. defeated Osgoode Hall. Wellington H. C. winners of tie.

Upper Canada College defeated Trinity University; Victoria H. C. of Toronto defeated Toronto University; Upper Canada College defeated Victoria H. C. of Toronto. Upper Canada College winners of tie.

Guelph H. C. defeated Galt H. C.; Berlin H. C. defeated Galt H. C.; Guelph H. C. defeated Berlin H. C. Guelph H. C. winners of tie.

Brampton H. C. defeated Victoria H. C. of Hamilton (by default). Brampton H. C. winners of tie.

London H. C. defeated St. Mary's H. C. London H. C. winners of tie.

Listowell H. C. defeated Stratford H. C. Listowell H. C. winners of tie.

SECOND ROUND.

Peterboro H. C. defeated Frontenac H. C.   Peterboro H. C. winners of tie.
Wellington H. C. defeated Upper Canada College.   Wellington H. C. winners of tie.
Guelph H. C. defeated Brampton H. C., 9 to 2.   Guelph H. C. winners of tie.
Listowell H. C. defeated London H. C.   Listowell H. C. winners of tie.

THIRD ROUND.

Wellington H. C. defeated Peterboro H. C., 6 to 3.   Wellington H. C. winners of tie.
Guelph H. C. defeated Listowell H. C.   Guelph H. C. winners of tie.

FINAL ROUND.

Wellington H. C...............defeated Guelph H. C............. 6 to 3
Guelph H. C..................   "   Wellington H. C......... 5 to 4

Wellington H. C. winning Junior Championship.......... ......10 to 8

&

THE STANLEY CUP.

The Stanley Cup, which is emblematic of the ice hockey championship of the world, was presented for competition by Lord Stanley, late Governor-General of Canada.

Up to February, 1896, this championship trophy had always been held by the team winning the senior championship of the Amateur Hockey League of Canada.   During the month named the Victoria Hockey Club of Winnipeg, champions of the Manitoba and Northwest Amateur Hockey Association, challenged the holders of this cup, the Victoria Hockey Club of Montreal, and as a result one of the greatest exhibitions of ice hockey ever played took place in Montreal on February 14, 1896.

As may be imagined, the undertaking of such a task by the Victorias of Winnipeg was a matter of no small account, when it is borne in mind that the distance from Winnipeg to Montreal is something over 1,500 miles, and the trip (over Canadian railways) occupies the greater part of three days.   That this team was probably the greatest and most skilful that ever played the game is proved by the fact that after a most trying journey and before a wildly excited assemblage of thousands of bitter enemies, they defeated the renowned and supposed invincible Victoria Hockey Club of Montreal by a score of two goals to none. The teams lined up for this memorable match as follows:

VICTORIAS OF WINNIPEG	POSITIONS	VICTORIAS OF MONTREAL
Merritt	Goal	Jones
Fleet	Point	Henderson
Higginbotham	Cover-Point	Grant, Captain
Armytage, Captain		Macdougall
Bain	Forwards	Wa lace
Howard		McLea
Campbell		Davidson

The two goals were scored by the Winnipeg team during the first twenty minutes of play, by such wonderful combination and team work as had rarely been exhibited to Montreal audiences. Captain Armytage then decided to save his men until further effort was necessary, and for the remainder of the hour of playing time worked his team wholly on the defensive. It may be understood what a marvelous defense Winnipeg had in Higginbotham, Fleet and Merritt, from the fact that during this last forty minutes, dozens of fierce attempts by the Montreal " Vics " to break through and score proved fruitless. Higginbotham was the hero of the match, and his brilliant work caused•him to be pronounced by unbiased critics the greatest cover-point that ever played ice hockey. Time after time his wonderful lifting and dribbling sent the puck far from his goal and practically caused the downfall of the Victorias of Montreal.

*　ˋ*　*　*　*　*　*　*

Last winter (during December, 1896) the Victoria Hockey Club of Montreal, ex-holders of the Stanley Cup, issued a challenge to the Victoria Hockey Club of Winnipeg for the possession of the trophy, which the latter club had so gallantly won the winter previous. The trustees of the cup ordered the Winnipeg "Vics" to defend it and their title of Ice Hockey Champions of the World, on the evening of December 30, 1896.

The match was played in Winnipeg, and after a very close and highly exciting contest the Montreal team regained the cup and honors, winning by a score of six goals to five. Like the previous contest for the Stanley Cup, this was a wonderful exhibition of the game, fast and clean from start to finish and marked by the accurate shooting for goals and combination work of both forward lines, which was simply grand, being remarkably rapid and sure.

The very close score would prove the claim of the Winnipeg team that their defeat was caused by their greatly weakened defense, owing to the loss of the valuable services of the great Higginbotham, who was accidentally killed in September, 1896, by a fall from a horse. Johnston, who filled this renowned cover-point's position, played as well and sure as could be expected, but of course lacked the long experience of Higginbotham. The players and their positions were as follows :

VICTORIAS OF WINNIPEG	POSITIONS	VICTORIAS OF MONTREAL
Merritt	Goal	Lewis
Fleet	Point	Henderson
Johnston	Cover-Point	Grant, Captain
Armytage, Captain		Macdougall
Bain	Forwards	Drinkwater
Howard		McLea
Campbell		Davidson

The Winnipeg team had the best of the match in the first half and seemed sure winners, the half ending four goals to two in their favor. They shot three goals before the visiting team got their eyes open, the first being scored in six minutes of play, the second in two and the third in ten. Then, after five minutes, Montreal scored her first goal, adding another in six minutes, and, just as half time was called, the Winnipegs scored their fourth tally.

The forwards of the home team had played perfectly, but the pace had been too much for them, and during the last half they showed signs of weakness due to over-training. On the contrary, the Montreal players seemed stronger, and by brilliant rushes of their forwards soon tied the score. A fierce struggle followed and the excitement was at fever heat. Finally one of the Montreal forwards secured the puck in the open and made a rush the entire length of the rink, dodging three opponents and scoring a beautiful goal, making the score five to four in his team's favor.

The Winnipeg " Vics " responded to the great support of their admirers and, pulling themselves together for a final effort, played fast and furious hockey, and, after a grand piece of combination play, scored a goal, which again tied the score.

With but five minutes' playing time remaining the excitement grew intense. Winnipeg's great effort in scoring their last goal told upon them, and as they faced off for the finish they presented a much worn appearance. Montreal went at the game with renewed effort and scored the winning goal after playing four minutes, making the final score six to five, and the world's championship was once more won and lost, and the Stanley Cup, so grandly won by the Winnipeg "Vics" the previous season, went back to its former stand in the club rooms of the Victoria Hockey Club of Montreal.

PLAYING AND CHAMPIONSHIP RULES OF ICE HOCKEY

OF THE

Amateur Hockey League of New York

AMENDED NOVEMBER, 1897.

❧

ICE HOCKEY RULES.

RULE I.

Team.—A team shall be composed of seven players, who shall be *bona-fide* members of the club they represent.

RULE II.

Game.—The game shall be commenced and renewed by a face in the centre of the rink. Rink shall be at least 112 feet by 58 feet.

RULE III.

Goals.—A goal is placed in the middle of each goal line, composed of two upright posts, four feet in height, placed six feet apart, and at least five feet from the end of the ice. The goal posts shall be firmly fixed. In the event of a goal post being displaced or broken, the Referee shall blow his whistle, and the game shall not proceed until the goal is replaced.

RULE IV.

Face.—The puck shall be faced by being placed between the sticks of two opponents, and the Referee then calling play.

RULE V.

Match.—Two halves of twenty minutes each, exclusive of stoppages, with an intermission of ten minutes between, will be the time allowed for games. A game will be decided by the team scoring the greatest number of goals during that time. In case of a tie after playing the specified time, play will continue for ten minutes more, when, in the event of the score still being even, another game will be played at a time and place mutually agreed upon, such time to be prior to the next scheduled game. Goals shall be changed after each half.

RULE VI.

Change of Players.—No change of players shall be made after a game has commenced, except for reasons of accidents or injury during the game.

RULE VII.

Should any player meet with an accident during a game and be compelled to leave the ice, his side shall have the option of putting on a spare man from the reserve to equalize the teams. In the event of any dispute between the captains as to such player's fitness to continue the game, the matter shall at once be decided by the Referee.

RULE VIII.

Stoppages.—Should a game be temporarily stopped by the infringement of any of the rules, the captain of the opposite team may claim that the puck be taken back and a face take place where it was last played from before such infringement occurred.

RULE IX.

Off-Side.—When a player hits the puck, any one of the same side who at such moment of hitting is nearer the opponent's goal line is off-side, and may not touch the puck himself or in any way whatever prevent any other player from doing so until the puck has been played. A player must always be on his own side of the puck.

RULE X.

Knocking on, Charging, Etc.—The puck may be stopped, but not carried or knocked on, by any part of the body. No player shall raise his stick above the shoulder. Charging from behind, tripping, collaring, kicking or cross-checking shall not be allowed, and the Referee must rule off the ice, for any time in his discretion, a player who, in his opinion, has offended deliberately against the above rule.

.RULE XI.

Puck Off Ice.—When the puck goes off the ice behind the goal line, or a foul occurs behind the goal line, the puck shall be brought out by the Referee to a point five yards in front of the goal line, at right angles from the point at which it left the ice, and there faced. When the puck goes off the ice at the side it shall be similarly faced three yards from the side.

RULE XII.

Goal-keeper.—The goal-keeper must not, during play, lie, kneel or sit upon the ice, but must maintain a standing position.

RULE XIII.

Score.—A goal shall be scored when the puck shall have passed between the goal posts from in front and below an imaginary line across the top of posts.

RULE XIV.

Sticks.—Hockey sticks shall be made of wood, with no harder substance attached thereto, and shall not be more than three inches wide at any point.

RULE XV.

Puck.—The puck must be made of vulcanized rubber, one inch thick all through and three inches in diameter.

RULE XVI.

Officials.—The captains of the contesting teams shall agree upon a Referee, a Timekeeper and two Umpires, one to be stationed behind each goal, which positions shall not be changed during a game except by mutual consent.

RULE XVII.

Referee.—All disputes on the ice shall be settled by the Referee, and his decision shall be final.

RULE XVIII.

Umpires.—All questions as to goals shall be settled by the Umpires, and their decisions shall be final.

&

CHAMPIONSHIP RULES.

RULE I.

The season shall be between December 1 and April 1.

RULE II.

The championship shall be decided by a series of games, a schedule of which shall be arranged at the annual meeting. The club winning the most games shall be declared champions.

RULE III.

All championship games shall be played on covered rinks, arranged for at the annual convention.

RULE IV.

The League shall offer a championship trophy, the winning club to hold same and be recognized as champions.

RULE V.

Any team making default shall forfeit its right to compete for the championship for that season, and all games played by defaulting team shall be declared off.

RULE VI.

A Referee should be decided upon by the captains forty-eight hours before a game.

RULE VII.

It shall be the duty of the captains of the contesting teams to hand to the Referee the names of the players for each game before the start. It shall be the duty of the Referee to forward to the Secretary of the League the score of each game, with the names of players and umpires.

RULE VIII.

Captains before a game shall toss for choice of goals.

RULE IX.

A player must be a *bona-fide* member of the club he represents at least thirty (30) days before he is eligible to compete in championship games. No player shall play in an Amateur Hockey League schedule game who, during the then current season, has played with another club in a recognized Hockey Association, without special permission of the Executive.

RULE X.

All clubs must register with the Secretary of the League the colors of their playing uniform, and no two clubs shall be permitted to have uniforms of the same color. The order of being admitted to League membership shall determine choice of colors.

LAWS AND CHAMPIONSHIP RULES OF ICE HOCKEY

AMENDED DECEMBER, 1896,

BY THE

Amateur Hockey Association of Canada

❧

LAWS OF ICE HOCKEY.

RULE I.

Team.—A team shall be composed of seven players, who shall be *bona-fide* members of the clubs they represent. No player shall be allowed to play on more than one team in the same series during a season, except in a case of *bona-fide* change of residence.

RULE II.

Game.—The game shall be commenced and renewed by a face in the centre of the rink. Rink must be at least 112 feet by 58 feet.

RULE III.

Goals—Goals shall be six feet wide and four feet high.

RULE IV.

Face.—The puck shall be faced by being placed between the sticks of two opponents, and the Referee then calling "play." The goals shall be placed at least ten feet from the edge of the ice.

RULE V.

Match.—Two half hours, with an intermission of ten minutes between, will be the time allowed for matches, but no stops of more than fifteen minutes will be allowed. A match will be decided by the team winning the greatest number of *games during that time. In case of a tie after playing the specified two half hours, play will continue until one side secures a *game, unless otherwise agreed upon between the captains before the match. Goals shall be changed after each half hour.

RULE VI.

Change of Players.—No change of players shall be made after a match has commenced, except for reasons of accidents or injury during the game.

RULE VII.

Should any player be injured during a match and compelled to leave the ice, his side shall have the option of putting on a spare man from the reserve to equalize the teams. However, should a player be injured during the second half, the captain of the opposing team shall have the option of dropping a man to equalize the teams or allow his opponents to put on a spare man. In the event of any dispute between the captains as to the injured player's fitness to continue the game, the matter shall at once be decided by the Referee.

RULE VIII.

Stoppages.—Should a game be temporarily stopped by the infringement of any of the rules, the captain of the opposite team may claim that the puck be taken back and a face take place where it was last played from before such infringement occurred.

RULE IX.

Off-Side.—When a player hits the puck, any one of the same side who at such moment of hitting is nearer the opponent's goal line is out of play, and may not touch the puck himself or

---

* NOTE BY EDITOR.—The word game or games in the instances thus marked means goal or goals, being a common expression among Canadian hockeyists for what Americans term a goal or score.

in any way whatever prevent any other player from doing so until the puck has been played. A player must always be on his own side of the puck.

RULE X.

Knocking on, Charging, Etc.—The puck may be stopped, but not carried or knocked on, by any part of the body. No player shall raise his stick above his shoulder except in lifting the puck. Charging from behind, tripping, collaring, kicking or shinning shall not be allowed, and any player after having been warned by the Referee, he may rule the player off the ice for that *game or match, or for such portion of actual playing time as he may deem fit.

RULE XI.

Puck Off Ice.—When the puck goes off the ice or a foul occurs behind the goals it shall be taken by the Referee to five yards at right angles from the goal line and there faced. When the puck goes off the ice at the sides it shall be taken by the Referee to five yards at right angles from the boundary line and there faced.

RULE XII.

Goal-keeper.—The goal-keeper must not, during play, lie, kneel or sit upon the ice, but must maintain a standing position.

RULE XIII.

Score.—Goal shall be scored when the puck shall have passed between the goal posts from in front and below an imaginary line across the top of posts.

RULE XIV.

Sticks.—Hockey sticks shall not be more than three inches wide at any part.

RULE XV.

Puck.—The puck must be made of vulcanized rubber, one inch thick all through and three inches in diameter.

RULE XVI.

Officials.—The captains of the contesting teams shall agree upon a Referee and two Umpires (one to be stationed behind each goal), which positions shall not be changed during a match, and two Timekeepers. In the event of the captains failing to agree on Umpires and Timekeepers the Referee shall appoint same.

RULE XVII.

Referee.—All disputes on the ice shall be settled by the Referee, and his decision shall be final.

RULE XVIII.

Umpires.—All questions as to *games shall be settled by the Umpires, and their decisions shall be final. In the event of any dispute as to the decision of an Umpire the Referee shall have power to remove and replace him.

CHAMPIONSHIP RULES.

RULE I.

The season shall be from the 1st of January to the 8th of March, both days inclusive.

RULE II.

The championship shall be decided by a series of games, a schedule of which shall be drawn up by one delegate from each club at the annual convention. The club winning the most matches shall be declared champions.

RULE III.

All championship matches shall be played on rinks arranged for at the annual convention.

RULE IV.

No club shall be allowed to compete for the Senior Championship until it has won the Intermediate Championship and only by the unanimous vote of all the clubs then comprising the series. The following clubs are at present qualified to compete for the Senior Championship, viz.: Quebec, Ottawa, Shamrock, Victoria and Montreal.

RULE V.

The Association shall offer a championship trophy, the winning club to hold same and be recognized as Champions of

Canada.   The trophy shall be delivered to the winning club
within seven days after the close of the season.

RULE VI.

Any club holding the championship for three years in succession shall become absolute owners of the championship trophy.

RULE VII.

Any team making default shall forfeit its right to compete
for the championship for that season, in the class in which it
is entered, and be liable to a fine of $100, unless good reasons
can be given for defaulting.   All matches played by defaulting
team shall be declared off.

RULE VIII.

A man who has played in more than two Senior Championship matches in one season shall not be eligible to play for the
Intermediate Championship in the same season.

RULE IX.

In the event of any two clubs failing to agree upon a Referee
four days before a match, the President shall call a meeting of
delegates (one from each club), to be held in Montreal, with
the view of choosing a Referee for the match in question.
Such delegates shall have no other power than to select such
Referee for the match named.

RULE X.

It shall be the duty of the captains of the contesting teams
to hand to the Referee the names of the players for each match
previous to the start, on forms supplied by the Secretary of the
Association.   The Referee shall then fill in the date of the
match, names of contesting clubs, the score at the finish, with
the names of Umpires, the whole duly signed by himself and
forwarded to the Secretary of the Association.

NOTE BY EDITOR. —The playing rules governing the matches
played by the Manitoba and Northwest Amateur Hockey Association are practically the same as those used by the Amateur
Hockey Association of Canada, differing only in arrangement
and slight wording changes.

RULES OF ICE HOCKEY

OF THE

ONTARIO HOCKEY ASSOCIATION

As Adopted December 5, 1896.

✿

RULES OF THE GAME

RULE I.

Game.—The game is played on ice by teams of seven on each side, with a puck made of vulcanized rubber, one inch thick all through and three inches in diameter.

RULE II.

Sticks.—Hockey sticks shall not be more than three inches wide at any part and not more than thirteen inches long in the blade.

RULE III.

Goals.—A goal is placed in the middle of each goal line, composed of two upright posts four feet in height, placed six feet apart and at least five feet from the end of the ice. The goal posts shall be firmly fixed. In the event of a goal post being displaced or broken, the referee shall blow his whistle and the game shall not proceed until the post is replaced.

RULE IV.

Match.—Each side shall have a captain (a member of his team) who, before the match, shall toss for choice of goals. Each side shall play an equal time from each end. The duration of championship matches shall not be less than one hour, exclusive of stoppages. The team scoring the greater number of goals in that time shall be declared the winner of the match. If at the end of that time the game is a draw, ends shall be changed and the game continued for ten minutes, each side playing five minutes from each end with a rest of five minutes between, and if neither side has then scored a majority of *games, similar periods of ten minutes shall be played in the same way until one side shall have scored a majority of goals.

RULE V.

Timekeepers.—Timekeepers shall be appointed, one by each captain, to keep the time during match.

RULE VI.

Referee.—There shall be only one referee for a match, and in no case shall he belong to either of the competing clubs. He shall enforce the rules, adjudicate upon disputes or cases unprovided for by rule, appoint the goal umpires, control the timekeepers, keep the score, and at the conclusion of the match declare the result. The puck shall be considered in play until the referee stops the game, which he may do at any time, and which he must do at once when any irregularity of play occurs, by sounding a whistle. His decision shall be final.

RULE VII.

Score.—A goal shall be scored when the puck shall have passed between the goal posts from in front and below an imaginary line drawn across the tops of the posts.

RULE VIII.

Goal Umpires.—Goal umpires shall inform the referee when a goal is scored. Their decisions shall be final.

RULE IX.

Face.—The game shall be started and renewed by the referee calling "play," after having placed the puck on its larger surface on the ice, between the sticks of the two players, one from

---

* See note by editor on page 67.

each team, who are to face it. After a goal has been scored the puck shall be placed on the centre of the ice.

RULE X.

Off-Side.—A player shall always be on his side of the puck. A player is off-side when he is in front of the puck, or when the puck has been hit, touched or is being run with, by any of his own side behind him (*i. e.*, between himself and his own goal line). A player being off-side is put on-side when the puck has been hit by, or has touched the dress or person of any player of the opposite side, or when one of his own side has run in front of him, either with the puck or having played it when behind him. If a player when off-side plays the puck, or annoys or obstructs an opponent, the puck shall be faced where it was last played before the off-side play occurred.

RULE XI.

Knocking-on.—The puck may not be stopped with the hand except by the goal-keeper (see Rule XIV.), but may be stopped, but not carried or knocked on by any other part of the body.

RULE XII.

Charging, Tripping, Etc.—No player shall raise his stick above his shoulder. Charging from behind, tripping, collaring, kicking, cross-checking or pushing shall not be allowed. And the referee must rule off the ice, for any time in his discretion, a player who, in the opinion of the referee, has deliberately offended against the above rule.

RULE XIII.

When the Puck Leaves the Ice.—When the puck goes off the ice behind the goal line it shall be brought out by the referee to a point five yards in front of the goal line, on a line at right angles thereto, from the point at which it left the ice, and there faced. When the puck goes off the ice at the side, it shall be similarly faced three yards from the side.

RULE XIV.

Goal-keeper.—The goal-keeper must not during play, lie, sit or kneel upon the ice; he may, when in goal, stop the puck with his hands, but shall not throw or hold it. He may wear pads, but must not wear a garment such as would give him undue assistance in keeping goal. The referee must rule off the ice, for any time in his discretion, a player who, in the opinion of the referee, has offended deliberately against this rule.

RULE XV.

Change of Players.—No change of players shall be made after a match has commenced, except by reason of accident or injury during the game.

RULE XVI.

Injured Player.—Should any player be injured during a match and compelled to leave the ice, the opposite side shall always drop a man to equalize the teams. In event of any dispute between the captains, as to the injured player's fitness to continue the game, the matter shall . t once be decided by the referee.

RULE XVII.

Stoppages.—Should the game be stopped by the referee by reason of the infringement of any of the rules, or because of an accident or change of players, the puck shall be faced at the spot where it was last played before such infringement, accident or change of players shall have occurred.

ICE POLO

Ice polo is said to be a development from shinney, but as it is played almost exclusively in New England, and especially in and about Boston, it would seem nearer correct to credit its origin to the great and popular game of roller polo, which is played very extensively by leagues of professional clubs in Boston, Fall River, Providence, Salem, Pawtucket, New Bedford, Lynn, Worcester and many other Eastern towns.

The game is frequently and erroneously referred to as American ice hockey by Canadians and those in this country who are unacquainted with either game. In the method of play there is a vast difference in the two games (ice hockey and ice polo), though in the object sought there is a great similarity.

In ice polo a ball is used instead of a puck, and a much heavier and stouter stick is employed, but the cardinal point wherein these sports differ, is the absence of any rule forbidding off-side play in ice polo and the almost universal one-handed use of the ice polo stick. Consequently ice polo is a more open game, the field of players being continually separated and the tries-for-goal being made from passes from unlimited directions.

Five men constitute an ice polo team, as follows : One goal-tend, one half-back, one centre and two rushers. The rushers must be rapid skaters, adepts in dribbling and passing, as well as accurate goal shots. They are called upon to shoot the ball at the goal when it is shot to them at its swiftest, from one of their own team. The centre is a support for the rushers, and either tries for goal himself or passes the ball to the most available rusher. Generally these three men carry the ball

down the rink in a triangular formation, equilateral or with
the base of the triangle from the opposing goal, thus allowing
of continual passing, one to the other, when the man carrying
the ball is opposed. The half-back should be the most robust
man of the team, as he must block his opponent's rushes, being
the first defense man they meet in the run toward the goal
they attack. His is a most difficult position, as he must also
intercept the majority of the tries for the goal which he de-
fends. The goal-tend must be a cool but active player. He
should rarely leave his station and never except in the case of
a great emergency.

Though this game has been largely indulged in in past
winters, it is believed to be on the decline, due to the rapid
increase of the much more scientific game of ice hockey.

Harvard, Yale and Brown Universities, Boston and Tufts
Colleges and Massachusetts Institute of Technology have
played ice polo for several years, but last winter all took up
the Canadian game, which Yale was the first to introduce.

The Massachusetts Ice Polo League is the principal body
fostering the game. Its membership includes teams representing Newton, Waltham, Newton A. A., Tufts College, Dorches-
ter, Felton A. A., Wakefield, Roxbury A. C. and Cambridge
Ice Polo and Hockey team.

The latter team, which easily won the championship of the
League, is considered the strongest aggregation that ever
played ice polo, and is clearly entitled to championship honors
by the splendid record made last winter. They played the
following twenty-three matches without losing one :

CAMBRIDGE ICE POLO AND HOCKEY TEAM—RECORD OF ICE
POLO MATCHES—SEASON OF 1896–97.

Date.		Goals.		Goals.
Dec. 18—Cambridge		8	Salem	0
" 22—	"	4	Newton	0*
" 26—	"	9	Lowell A. A.	0
" 28—	"	1	Harvard University	0
Jan. 4—	"	7	Lawrence	0
" 7—	"	7	Brown University	2
" 8—	"	5	Woburn	0
" 9—	"	3	Waltham	0*

* Massachusetts Ice Polo League matches.

CAMBRIDGE RECORD—*Continued.*

Date.		Goals.		Goals.
Jan. 11—Cambridge		6	Lynn A. C.	0
" 14—	"	3	Boston College.	0
" 16—	"	12	Milton Academy	0
" 17—	"	3	Newton A. A.	1*
" 20—	"	5	Tufts College.	0*
" 21—	"	1	Dorchester.	0*
" 23—	"	1	Arlington.	1
" 25—	"	8	Tiger Roadsters	0
" 26—	"	7	Felton A. A.	1*
" 28—	"	4	Wakefield.	0*
" 30—	"	6	Roxbury A. C.	0*
Feb. 2—	"	5	Boylston A. C.	0
" 4—	"	5	Harvard Picked Team	0
" 6—	"	4	Cambridge H. and L. School.	0
" 10—	"	7	Brooklyn Ice Polo Team	0
Total		121	Total	5

* Massachusetts Ice Polo League matches.

The credit of the organization of the Cambridge Ice Polo and Hockey team belongs to W. E. Jewell, Jr., who is an enthusiastic skater and promoter of all amateur sports. His ice polo team was made up as follows: W. E. Jewell, Jr., Captain; H. A. Hopkins, N. Tobey, Howard Glidden, Mark Lyman and "Jack" Corbett.

*   *   *   *   *   *   *   *

The New England Skating Association Interscholastic Ice Polo League has done much to promote the sport among the schools in the past by offering for competition a handsome silver loving-cup. Many excellent matches have been played by the teams comprising this league, which included last winter the following: Melrose High School, Roxbury Latin School, Somerville High School, Cambridge High and Latin School and Boston English School. The championship was undecided last winter, as warm weather prevented the play-off of the tie between Cambridge High and Latin School and Melrose High School, neither of whom lost a match throughout the whole season.

In the Inter-Prep. School League the team of the Arlington High School outclassed all the others and even defeated the Cambridge High and Latin School team, of the larger school league, in an exhibition match.

The ice polo team representing Brown University for two or three years back has been a very strong one, and their team of last season was only surpassed by the Cambridge five, who defeated Brown by a score of seven goals to two. The Brown team had a long string of victories to their credit last season, among them being the game against the Montclair Athletic Club, played in New York City on February 3d, which resulted in Brown's favor by two goals to one. The players who composed the Brown team last season were as follows : Watson, Captain ; Purvear, Hunt, Chase, Merrimam and Barrows.

*   *   *   *   *   *   *   *

In the vicinity of New York City for the last two winters the bright and shining light of ice polo circles was the New York Ice Polo Club, which made its headquarters at the Ice Palace skating rink. During the winter of 1895–6 this team (then called the Ice Palace Polo Club) played twenty-four matches, twenty-two of which were victories. One of these defeats was registered by the Brown University team, the score being four goals to two. Last winter this team made a record equally as good. Of fifteen matches played thirteen were victories, one a tie match, and one ended in a dispute. The record follows :

NEW YORK ICE POLO CLUB—RECORD OF MATCHES—
SEASON OF 1896-97.

	Goals		Goals
New York Ice Polo Club	5	Sagamore Ice Polo Club	0
" " "	2	Passaic Ice Polo Club	1
" " "	5	St. Bartholomew A. C.	0
" " "	5	Passaic Ice Polo Club	0
" " "	8	New Rochelle Ice Polo Club	0
" " "	3	Capitols of Albany (N. Y.)	0
" " "	3	Brooklyn Ice Polo Team	1
" " "	4	Yonkers A. C.	0
" " "	1	Montclair A. C.	1
" " "	3	Clifton Ice Polo Team	0
" " "	3	Sagamore Ice Polo Team	0
" " "	1	Montclair A. C.	0*
" " "	6	Passaic Ice Polo Club	0
" " "	2	Brooklyn Ice Polo Team	1
" " "	5	Brooklyn Ice Polo Team	0
Total	56	Total	4

*But one-half played ; match ended in a dispute.

The last two matches played with the Brooklyn Ice Polo Team were contests for a handsome silver cup, emblematic of the Ice Polo Championship of Greater New York. The personnel of the New York team was as follows: B. Phillips, Cannoll, Maloney, Bowe, Lake, Banning, Haspenwall, Koehler, Tierney, A. Wood, S. Kelly, H. Kelly, Palmato and Hornfeck.

Among other teams about the metropolitan district last winter were the following: Brooklyn Ice Polo Team, Montclair A. C., St. Bartholomew A. C., United States Marine Corps Ice Polo Team, from the Brooklyn Navy Yard ; New Rochelle Ice Polo Club, Passaic Ice Polo Club, Yonkers A. C., Hastings Ice Polo Team, Pastime A. C., Huguenot A. C., Sagamore Ice Polo Team and Clifton Ice Polo Team.

PLAYING RULES OF ICE POLO

AS ADOPTED BY THE

New England Skating Association

❧❧❧

1. Each team shall consist of five plays, as follows: one goal-tend, one half back, one centre, two rushers.

2. The distance from goal to goal shall be 150 feet. The goal shall be four feet wide.

3. The regulation Spalding ·Rubber Covered Polo Ball shall be used exclusively.

4. The sticks shall not exceed four feet in length nor one and one-fourth inches in diameter. Sticks shall have no material of any kind on them more than one foot from the top. No stringing of any kind is permissible.

5. The Referee shall examine the sticks of each player before the game begins.

6. Each Goal Umpire shall make a mark in some way on the goal tender eighteen inches from the ice, so that it may be seen plainly.

7. Time shall be taken out from the moment after a goal is made and the ball is placed in the centre to the moment when the sides are lined up ready to rush.

8. The time between halves shall not exceed ten minutes.

9. After each goal the ball shall be placed in the centre.

10. The Referee shall place the ball in the centre of the field between the two goals, and when both teams are lined up in their respective places, shall give the signal for play to begin.

11. In case of a skate coming off, or a serious accident, the Referee shall call ime and deduct time accordingly. Time shall not be called because a player drops or otherwise loses control of his stick.

12. No time exceeding five minutes shall be taken out for skate coming off or serious accident.

13. At the end of first half the sides shall change goals.

14. When time is called owing to loss of skate or serious injury, each player shall remain exactly where he was at the moment when time was called, and shall not move so that he cannot resume his exact location, until the Referee calls play.

15. In case of a tie the contesting teams shall play not to exceed ten minutes until one side makes a goal.

16. Should time be lengthened in above manner, in case of a serious accident or skate coming off, play must be resumed within two minutes.

17. A forfeited game shall count three goals to the side to whom the game is forfeited; nothing being allowed the opposite side.

18. For every three fouls which a side makes one goal shall be deducted.

19. A goal shall be considered as three (3) points.

20. In case of tie, the side which has made fewest fouls shall be declared the winner.

21. A postponed game or a tie game shall be played off as soon as the weather permits.

22. A goal is made by passing the ball over a straight line connecting the two elements of the goal at height from the ice of not more than eighteen inches.

23. There shall be two 20-minute halves.

24. It shall constitute a foul (1) if any player touches the ball with his hand; (2) if any player blocks off or holds; (3) if any player purposely trips another player; (4) if any player throws his stick at the ball; (5) if any player goes within the Goal-Tender's circle; (6) if any player kicks the ball into the goal; (7) if any player strikes the ball while his skate is off; (8) if any player drives the ball through the goal from the rear;

(9) if any player strikes the ball while any portion of his body is in contact with the ice.

25. The Goal-Tender's circle shall include the ice within a radius of two feet from the centre of the goal.

26. The duties of the Umpires shall be to decide if the ball goes within the required goal limits.

27. The duties of the Referee shall be to have general charge of the ball, to call time and to declare the fouls.

The decision of the Referee shall be final, and any club refusing to play the game out shall lose the game.

HOCKEY STICKS..

No. **XXX.** Hockey Stick, made of selected material, and in accordance with league regulations. Price, ... Each, **75c.**

No. **XX.** Hockey Stick, good quality material, regulation style. . . . . Each, **50c.**

PUCK

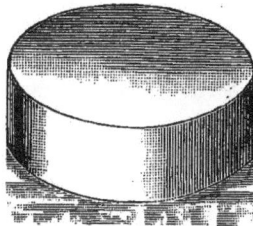

Made of best quality rubber.

Regulation size and weight.

No. **13.** Price, ... Each, **50c.**

Catalogue of Fall and Winter Sports Free

A. G. SPALDING & BROS.

NEW YORK   CHICAGO
PHILADELPHIA   WASHINGTON

CANADIAN PATTERN CLUB HOCKEY SKATE

Our Canadian Pattern Hockey Skate is endorsed by the Canadian Associations, and almost exclusively used by the leading hockey players. . . . . Per pair, **$5.00**

⚜⚜⚜

Peck & Snyder's Professional Racing Skate

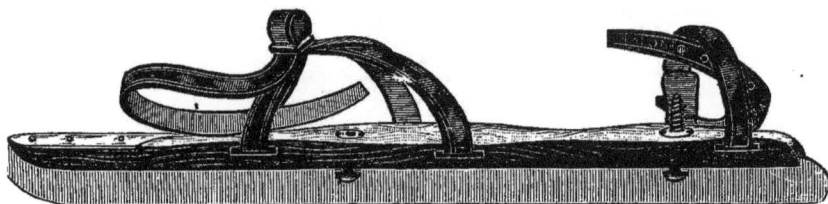

No. **5.** Polished mahogany tops, highest tempered steel runners, nickel-plated and handsomely polished, russet leather heel and toe straps. Made in three lengths, 14, 16 and 18 inches . . . . Per pair, **$5.00**

⚜⚜⚜

NEW AMERICAN CLUB SPEED SKATE
For Racing and Straightaway Skating

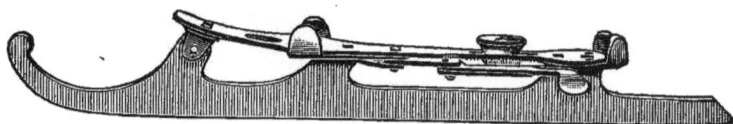

No. **E.** Cold rolled steel foot plates, extra quality steel clamps with spring temper, very best polished, welded and tempered steel runners, fitted with our new Sliding Clamp Adjustment, and electro-nickel-plated throughout. Runners, 14 to 17 inches. Sizes, 8½ to 12 inches. . Per pair, **$5.00**

Catalogue of Fall and Winter Sports Free

SPALDING'S INDIAN CLUBS.

Our Trade Mark Indian Clubs are of selected material and perfect in shape. They are finely polished, with ebonite centre band and gilt stripe top and bottom. Each pair wrapped in paper bag.

TRADE MARK CLUBS.

Weight.		Per Pair.
1-2 pound,	.	$ .40
3-4 "	.	.45
1 "	.	.50
1 1-2 "	.	.60
2 "	.	.70
2 1-2 "	.	.75
3 "	.	.80
4 "	.	1.00
5 "	.	1.25

WOOD DUMB BELLS.

Our Trade Mark Bells are made of selected material, neatly decorated, well finished and of perfect balance.

Weight.		Per Pair.
1-4 pound,	.	$ .35
1-2 "	.	.35
3-4 "	.	.45
1 "	.	.50
1 1-2 "	.	.60
2 "	.	.65
3 "	.	.85
4 "	.	1.00

Our complete Catalogue for all Athletic Sports, Uniforms and Gymnasium Goods mailed free to any address.

A. G. SPALDING & BROS.,

NEW YORK.   CHICAGO.   PHILADELPHIA.

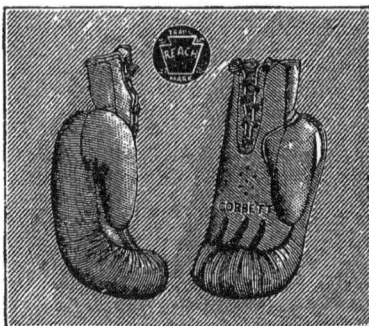

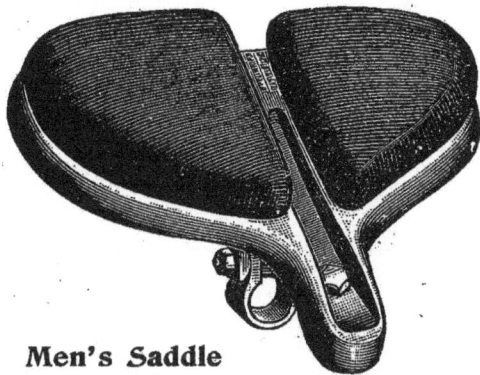

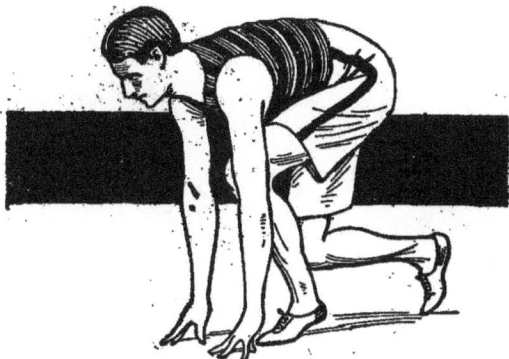

Spalding's Athletic Sweaters.....

Shaker Sweaters Made of selected American wool and of superior quality in fit and finish. Guaranteed to be absolutely all wool and full shaped to body and arms. Colors: White, Black, Navy Blue and Tan.

No. **3.**	Standard weight,	.	.	.	**$3.50**
No. **5.**	Lighter weight,	.	.	.	**2.50**

Ribbed Sweaters Our No. 9 Sweater is made of pure wool, full shaped to body and arms. It is guaranteed superior to any sweater of equal price.

No. **9.** Medium weight, . . . **$1.50**

Our No. 11 is not all wool, but contains more of it than most sweaters usually sold at a higher price as all wool sweaters.

No. **11.** Medium weight, . . . **$1.00**

TURTLE NECK PIECES FOR ALL STYLE SWEATERS

An extra protection for cold or raw weather. May be worn with a light sweater and affords the same protection. Colors: White, Navy, Black, Maroon. Special colors or stripes to order.

No. **15.** Solid colors, . . . **$1.25**
No. **20.** Striped to order, . . **1.50**

CATALOGUE of all Athletic Sports Mailed
∴ Free to any Address..........

A. G. Spalding & Bros.

New York   Chicago
Philadelphia
Washington

The Spalding
HIGHEST QUALITY

Athletic Sweaters

Our "Highest Quality" Sweaters are made of the very finest Australian lamb's wool and are exceedingly soft and pleasant to wear. They are full fashioned to body and arms and without seams of any kind. We call special attention to the "Intercollegiate" grade, which were originally made by special order for the Yale foot ball eleven and are now exclusively used by all Intercollegiate players. They are considerably heavier than the heaviest sweater ever knitted and cannot be furnished by any other maker, as we have exclusive control of this special weight. The various grades in our "Highest Quality" Sweaters are identical in quality and finish, the difference in price being due entirely to variations in weight. Colors: White, Navy Blue, Black and Maroon.

No. A.	"Intercollegiate," special weight,	$7.00
No. B.	Heavy weight, .	5.00
No. C.	Standard weight, .	4.50

Complete Catalogue of Athletic Uniforms and all other requisites for Indoor and Outdoor Sports mailed free to any address.

A. G. SPALDING & BROS.

New York   Chicago   Philadelphia   Washington

SPALDING'S ❧❧
STRIKING BAGS

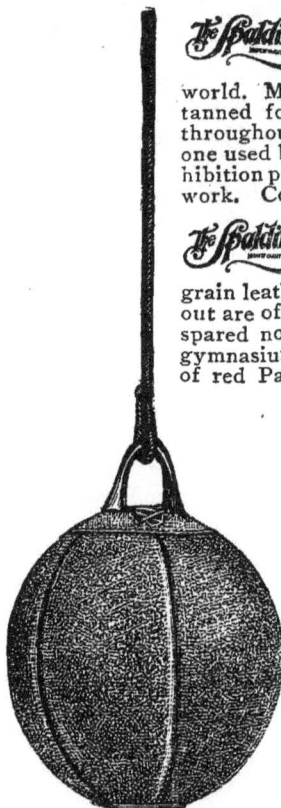

HIGHEST QUALITY CORBETT BAG. No. 18. Designed and endorsed by James J. Corbett, champion of the world. Made of the very finest grain leather, specially tanned for this bag, extra well and carefully made throughout, and each bag the exact duplicate of the one used by Champion Corbett in training and for exhibition purposes. Splendidly adapted for gymnasium work. Complete, in box.................**$10.00**

HIGHEST QUALITY GYMNASIUM BAG. No. 13. Made in regulation size and of the finest imported pebble grain leather; the sewing and workmanship throughout are of the most substantial character, and we have spared no expense in making this an ideal bag for gymnasium work. The bladder is of a special grade of red Para rubber, extra heavy, and made expressly for this bag. It is extremely lively and very durable. We recommend nothing cheaper in striking bags intended for gymnasium use. Packed complete, in box.............................**$8.00**

No. 12. THE STANDARD SPECIAL. Regulation size, made of selected oil tanned grain leather, silk stitched and carefully made. This bag is particularly adapted for quick work. Each bag complete in box..............................**$5.00**

No. 10. THE STANDARD. Regulation size, made of specially tanned glove leather, substantially put together. Each bag complete in box.............**$4.00**

No. 17. THE EXPERT. Regulation size, made of fine Napa leather and well finished. Each bag complete in box, **$3.50**

No. 16. THE PRACTICE. Medium size, fine grain leather cover and well made throughout. Each bag complete in box...................**$2.50**

EXTRA BLADDERS.

No. A. For Corbett Bag No. 18 and Gymnasium Bag No. 13. Extra fine quality rubber and expressly made for these bags...........**$1.25**

No. B. For Bags Nos. 12, 10 and 17. Fine quality rubber and very durable...**$1.00**

No. C. For Bag No. 16.....................................**75c.**

A. G. SPALDING & BROS., New York. Chicago. Philadelphia.

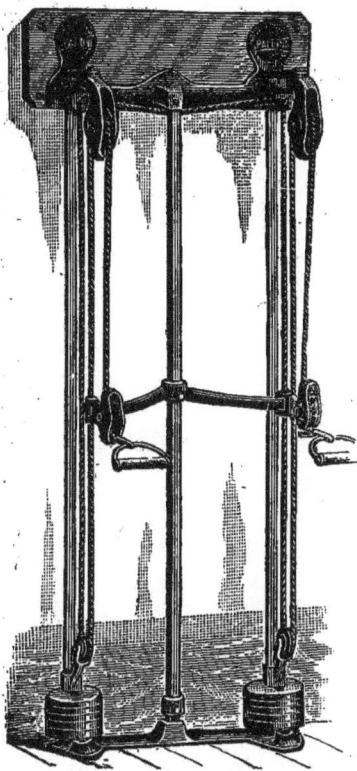